ETA

A BOMBER COMMAND NAVIGATOR
SHOT DOWN AND ON THE RUN
GORDON MELLOR

ETA

Published in 2016 by Fighting High Ltd,
www.fightinghigh.com

Copyright © Fighting High Ltd, 2016
Copyright text © Gordon Mellor, 2016

British Library Cataloguing-in-Publication data.
A CIP record for this title is available from the
British Library.

ISBN – 13: 978-0993415258

Designed and typeset in Adobe Minion 11/15pt
by Michael Lindley, www.truthstudio.co.uk.

Printed and bound in the UK by Gomer Press.
Front cover design by www.truthstudio.co.uk.

Contents

Now Hear This

Hello,

I am glad that your curiosity has prompted you to be with me now at the beginning of this memoir, and I hope that you can accompany me right through this story to the last page.

On a number of occasions it has been suggested that I put my recollections down on paper. Well now I have done so and covered a period of some six years. I was encouraged to pen these words by Lawrie Walford of the RAF Lichfield Association, who wanted to add them to their records. In addition I was further encouraged by being asked to record an audio contribution to the Imperial War Museum archive, followed by some supporting pressure from within my own family. But, principally, I wrote this chronicle to recognise how extraordinary were the ordinary people of the countries of Europe that were occupied by the armed forces of the Nazi regime at a time when supporters of the Allies faced the ultimate penalty.

What follows is a ramble through times, personal events and reflections, most of which involved relationships with many other persons in service with the Royal Air Force from 1939, when this country and France prepared for a conflict with the German nation, until my return to civilian life in 1946. It is viewed after a delay of more than sixty years, which in the early days after the war we all had hoped would be of peace. But they haven't been, have they?

As might be expected, the content of the story contains a stronger male element than perhaps would be presumed now in a new century where women have an expanding influence on all walks of life and in particular on both military and civilian aviation. In this account there is a period where the balance is reversed and women of our Allies dominate the scene. Can one ever forget what amazing women they were, and today there are still a few survivors.

The title of this book, just three letters – ETA – are of course an abbreviation for 'Estimated Time of Arrival', frequently used these days by the great travelling public, but at the time of this narrative it was used mainly by flying crews. ETA was of prime importance to navigators and pilots, for operational planning was timed to the minute. Also it was always of great interest to all of the aircrew. One could say that our lives depended on time and timing. As a matter of fact I am sure it was the most frequent question asked of a navigator when he was working, even more so perhaps than 'Where are we?' Among many crews it was a standing joke to say that 'The Nav' was the last person to find out our position. The occasional quip and a laugh at the right time was good for all, but confidence in each of your crew's ability in their particular role was always absolute, as was evident on the occasions of returning to this Britain in the cold light of dawn to find the ground obscured with fog.

It was a great job to do.

APPLICATION FOR ENROLMENT

This application should be completed and detached, folded as directed overleaf, and posted to or left at the appropriate address as shown in the Guide. (If posted no stamp is required.)

SECTION 1 — For use by Applicant.

(1) Surname ___Mr. MELLOR.___

(IN BLOCK LETTERS and stating whether Mr., Mrs. or Miss)

(2) Christian names ___GORDON. HERBERT.___

(3) Age ___19 YRS 5 MONTHS___

(4) Full home address ___13, DOUGLAS AVENUE,___
___WEMBLEY,___
___MIDDLESEX___

(5) Service which it is desired to enter ___
___ROYAL AIR FORCE VOLUNTEER RESERVE___
___AIRCRAFT CREW SECTION (AIR OBSERVERS)___

(6) Present occupation ___
___WORKER-UP FOR QUANTITY SURVEYORS.___

(7) Usual occupation if different from that shown in item (6)
___AS IN (6)___

(8) If employed, state Employer's name and address (if own employer, state " on own account ").

___MESSRS STEPHENSON, ELWELL AND KNIGHT.___
___38, PARLIAMENT STREET. S.W.1.___

(9) Employer's business ___QUANTITY SURVEYOR___

Signature of applicant ___Gordon H. Mellor___

SECTION II — For official use by the Ministry of Labour.

Occupational sub-Classification No. ___1433___

Decision as regards Occupation :
(a) Applicant may be enrolled.

(b) Applicant may be enrolled only in the capacity of ___

(c) Applicant may not be enrolled.

Signature of M/L Officer ___Polney___
Date ___5 MAY 1939___

FURTHER COPIES OF THIS FORM CAN BE OBTAINED AT ANY POST OFFICE OR LOCAL OFFICE OF THE MINISTRY OF LABOUR.

RAF Volunteer Reserve application May 1939.

Chapter 1

Name, Rank and Number

All was dark, not a spot of light to be seen anywhere. What time was it? Not that it really mattered. Must be early; I felt that I could easily drop off again for an hour or two until it was daylight. That was strange, I thought I could hear someone snoring gently. But I was warm and comfortable where I was, so that's fine.

A door crashed open; briefly a figure was silhouetted against the dim light behind, then strong lights sprang to life in this enormous room and a loud voice was shouting: 'Everybody up. Wakey wakey.' What was I doing here for goodness sake? A careful look into this brilliance revealed a figure in a blue uniform with sergeant's stripes on the sleeves of his jacket. Reality flooded in and I remembered why I was here with all these young men – although some looked more like boys. They had, as I had, all volunteered to fly in the Royal Air Force (RAF) for as long as required.

This all started with the return of the British prime minister, Mr Neville Chamberlain, from Munich in September 1938 after his conversations with the German chancellor, Adolf Hitler, and the display of the paper agreement to the media. The country realised that a conflict was probable. All that it had gained was a breathing space. Expansion of the armed forces was put in hand and each of the services appealed for volunteers to join the Territorial Army or the Auxiliary and Volunteer Reserves of the Navy and the RAF. The young men and women of the country responded.

My interest in aviation sprang from early visits to air shows at Hendon and Northolt, together with watching aircraft at the airfield adjoining the De Havilland aircraft factory at Stag Lane, Edgware. Also from being perched in a tree with school friends, overlooking the security fence at RAF Hendon.

In 1939 at the age of nineteen, with the possibility of flying within reach, the old enthusiasm returned. I was employed in the surveying profession, and air navigation appealed to me to the extent that I applied to the Royal Air Force Voluntary Reserve (RAFVR) to train as an observer. As aircraft crews at that time were small in number it appeared that the observer had to be able to carry out a variety of activities that could not be performed by the pilot while in control of the aircraft. Of course, many like-minded young men had the same idea and you had to await your turn for interview with the Air Ministry Assessment Board.

My first application came to grief during the early months of 1939 on medical grounds, but following many early morning exercise runs before leaving for work during spring and summer I applied again.

War was declared on Sunday, 3 September 1939 and I was very disappointed when my second application forms were returned in the post. Obviously a new approach had to be found.

My third attempt to join the RAF in 1940 was successful in part. The interviews and medical requirements were satisfied and, having been tested all in one morning, I was to find that there was a waiting period before aircrew training could commence. All candidates in that category were being sent home on deferred service.

Before this waiting period had amounted to more than just a few weeks I was recalled to help fill the need for ground defence of vulnerable airfields. In a short while I was entering the gates of No. 1 Depot Uxbridge and was here in company with many other young men with the same purpose.

The first few days were an eye opener for us all, particularly to those who had come from quite distant towns and countryside. To them the regular German air raids with the accompanying defence bombardment at night over central London was another new experience to be borne. The main adjustment to be made was that of accepting living in a barrack-room environment with some twenty other men and the consequent loss of all personal privacy. Of course, everyone understood that it was inevitable. The kitting out, the many inoculations, the square-bashing days and the initial friendship-making passed. Postings were the talk of the moment. For those of us in Mons barrack block it was to be to RAF Bridgnorth. Where was it situated? One of my new friends, John Wilkin, had worked for the Post Office service and knew that it was in Shropshire. Civilian clothing had been sent home, and all that we now possessed was being worn or packed into a kitbag and then we were off through the main gate. For myself, I was to return only once, years later.

The journey ended at the entrance to a vast encampment of wooden buildings, row upon row, side by side and end to end with several large parade grounds. We entered the main gate and were met with 'Get fell in, in three ranks', 'Right turn, quick march', 'Left, right, left. Swing those arms.' We were here to be changed from new recruits to the RAF's standard idea of airmen, with a hope that it was not to change each one's individuality.

Once or twice our flight was required to take on the role of camp security for the night. Two hours on, two hours off duty. Rifles were issued for the purpose; no ammunition of course, we were still raw recruits – some still had difficulty in knowing their right hand from their left on the parade ground.

After church parade on Sunday morning the day was free. On one such day, with a fine afternoon, four of us newcomers decided to walk into Bridgnorth town to see whatever it had to offer a visitor. The sightseeing did not progress very far for we found out that this was the day that local church and community groups provided afternoon tea and cake to off-duty servicemen. That was us clearly. The ladies at various meeting places were charming and the home-made cake delicious.

This initial training course was intended to last for four weeks but, at the end of the third week of square bashing, new postings were to hand and a number of us were to travel across the country to north Norfolk, to a well-established base at RAF Bircham Newton. On arrival we were directed to a large building attached to the side of one of the hangars; it had previously been used as the gymnasium. The floor of this vast echoing space was a sea of bed boards. Each set comprised three boards about 10in wide, supported at foot and head by wood rests to raise the bed about 6in off the floor, and was furnished with three or four blue-grey blankets. The luxury of a mattress, sheets and pillows had to be forgotten and realisation of the term 'hard lying' was obvious. The pay usually associated with that term was to prove absent.

On the morning after arrival a parade of the newcomers was held. Some forty of us in all. Volunteers for various jobs were called for; the vacancies were in the coal yard, the cookhouse, rubbish collection, the barber's shop and many more, none of which appealed to my five companions and myself. The numbers remaining diminished until there were just us six left. The sergeant's response was, 'Attention, right turn, quick march, halt, fall out.' And there we were outside the armoury. It became apparent that we were now part of the ground defence force – in fact other than the NCOs we were it, this being the very job that we had been called up to do until the aircrew training course became available.

As a variation to routine defence duty around the airfield an occasional visit to the lonely and isolated shoreline of Brancaster Bay to the north of Bircham was welcome. There a big kite would be assembled and flown to lift a large sleeve drogue high into the sea breeze to provide a target for training purposes. A mounting for machine guns was sited on the beach and practice with live 'ammo' against the wheeling and dipping drogue certainly improved one's reaction rapidly, but increase in the number of hits came more slowly until one got one's eye in. A breath of salt sea air was a great rejuvenator.

The weeks passed and the weather deteriorated. The frosty winds whistled across the flat airfield and the surrounding open countryside, making the duty period in the perimeter gun pits of two hours on and two hours off much less pleasurable than during the warmer days of summer and autumn. As an alternative position to the gun pits an Hispano cannon had been mounted on a lorry as mobile defence. No protection from the wind here. However, these duties provided us with the opportunity to become familiar with a wide range of weapons, which was to be of great value later in our service.

Many aircraft used Bircham Newton airfield. Not only the resident squadrons but also many planes returning from raids in difficulties found it to be conveniently situated for an emergency landing. In normal circumstances, other than using the perimeter track, walking on the airfield was forbidden, but one plane landed in an accessible area and of course those of us who could went to have a look. It was not quite what

I expected to see. The rear turret Perspex panels were shattered and the inside was red with much blood. An air gunner unknown to us had just paid a heavy price. From this moment, this was no longer an adventure but a conflict with serious consequences.

Shortly before Christmas 1940 we were recalled to the training programme of observer/navigator, initially for two weeks at Stratford-upon-Avon Reception Centre to make up a course number of fifty pupils. Then on to No. 6 Initial Training Wing (ITW) at Aberystwyth for basic training on a wide range of matters in addition to air navigation. We were lodged in a combined pub/hotel named the Lion Royal, and in my own case shared a fair-sized room with four other airmen. Out of a mixed group of young men only one, George Standring, had a service background, having been a trooper in the Royal Horse Guards.

Some three or four weeks after we had arrived at Aberystwyth and settled into the accommodation, John Wilkin, one of our room-mates and one who I had known since day one at Uxbridge, began to have difficulty in walking and general movement, which affected his prompt attendance on the course. So much so, that one morning before breakfast he was unable to move out of bed. This had gone on long enough; we rang sick quarters for an ambulance. In a very few minutes he was gone, kit and all.

The morning proceeded as normal with lectures. But this time not for long. The officer in charge of the course appeared and the four of us who shared the room with John were whisked away into isolation in a small hotel on the seafront. Everything from our room in the Lyon Royal was taken to the new quarters where we, as the sole occupants, could spread ourselves out a little. Food was to come in from sick quarters close by. Course work, to be completed regularly, was also to be delivered and we could take exercise, walks or runs, but no contact with other airmen or members of the public was allowed.

The reason for all this? It was considered that we were close contacts of a suspected case of a form of meningitis. Five or six days later it was all over. John was still in the isolation hospital at Tan-y-Bwlch but not with the suspected meningitis. We could visit him and did so when there was time. For us it was back to the Lion Royal with all our gear. At least we had enjoyed our exercise walks on the fine afternoons.

Keeping fit was a major consideration, with regular periods set aside for this purpose. Many Saturday afternoons saw a number of us engaged in the inter-squadron cross-country races. Out through the town, followed by a mile or two on the country roads and open ground, down to the edge of the sea near Tan-y-Bwlch along a stony track, across the bridge over the river and back to the seafront to the finish. The more often we ran the easier it became. Sergeant Brown was the senior NCO to the flight and had a corporal to assist who had been a Welsh national rugby player; consequently, our alternative sports activity had a strong rugby flavour. The corporal's running speed across the playing field turf was phenomenal, I had never run so fast before in my attempt to keep up with him and at that time I was no slouch at running. Even so, it seemed as if my feet never touched the ground.

The twelve-week period was one of constant effort, with regular tests and culminating in examinations across the board. Successful? Oh yes, but where do we go from here? The issue of tropical kit set the imaginations whirling. Rhodesia was a popular destination guess, plus one or two alternatives that were less practical. Administration was not saying. Seven days' leave was welcome.

Two weeks followed and were filled as if we were still on the course; however, a little light relief was to hand. Early one Sunday morning the whole course piled into a coach and we were off. The driver dropped us off at the edge of the road in the bottom of a steep valley, close to a rugged footpath that went uphill beside a stream. Flight Lieutenant Dickie, the course commander, led the way up at quite a pace for he had obviously done this climb before. Eventually the rocky ground levelled out and we approached a still, dark lake with the rough track skirting its edge. The spectacular views that we had observed during the first stage were disappearing as the cloud base had quickly come down and the tops of the hills in a horseshoe shape around the lake were now obscured. But nobody thought of turning back and again the eager airmen, in Indian file, climbed the remaining height to the top of Cadair Idris in thick mist. One was grateful for the extra clothing that had been carried all the way up.

The descent was by a different route, which led us down to Tal-y-llyn; there we were glad to see the coach outside the pub awaiting the party's return. What a brilliant piece of planning. There were quite stringent rules on the serving of drinks in Wales on a Sunday, but we did not seem to have much trouble in convincing the landlord that we were bona fide travellers with the dust of the road on our shoes. Then came a restful ride back to the Lion Royal in Aberystwyth. The whole enterprise had relieved us all of any spare energy that had been present at breakfast time.

Postings were up on the noticeboard and we were off to the holding depot at RAF Wilmslow. All one's possessions were hurriedly thrust into kit-bags; was it all there? No! What about that stuff at the laundry around the corner? A quick visit to collect my shirts and a last chance to say good-bye to the Chinese girls behind the counter who spoke English with a strong Welsh accent. Goodbye to all, including the young lady with whom I had spent many a pleasant evening. Aberystwyth was left behind with a few regrets for it had been a happy place, but it was with anticipation and desire to start the next phase in getting ourselves airborne. Apparently the post-ing to Wilmslow was to allow for sufficient numbers to be assembled for the next stage of our journey. A few days following our arrival and it was off again by train through the night – to where? After a disturbed sleep overnight and with the increasing brightness of daylight came the smell of salt air as we pulled into the dockside station at Gouroch on the Clyde. It was 4 April 1941.

A packet-boat named the *Royal Ulsterman* was moored alongside, and we went aboard with all our gear. Rumours again. Not Northern Ireland surely. Not with that issue of tropical kit at Aberystwyth in the bottom of my kitbag. The ship pulled away from the dockside and off down the firth of Clyde. Now that we, the passengers, were out of contact with the shore, our destination of Canada was revealed. But wasn't this rather a small ship for the North Atlantic?

During the night we had rounded the Mull of Kintyre and in the morn-ing were sailing up past Skye with the snow-covered hills of mainland Scotland on one side and those of the Outer Hebrides on the other. It was cold on deck, very cold; it was the view that took your breath away. At mealtimes airmen were required to line up on deck with mess tins and mugs ready to be filled with food and tea. Everything but the tea went into the mess tins – sweet and savoury together, to be carried quickly into the warmth of below decks to be consumed. In due course, on another grey morning, the *Royal Ulsterman* slipped into the cold waters of the harbour of Reykjavik in Iceland closely followed by our naval escort of one destroyer. What now?

Soon airmen with kitbags were passing down the gangway steps on to a transporter vessel and being taken across the harbour to a large passenger boat waiting there. We were to discover that it was named the *Derbyshire* and had been converted into an armed merchant cruiser. On this occasion it was also to serve as a military transport for us.

Former passenger accommodation in the cabins of the *Derbyshire* was already occupied by the Navy personnel manning the ship. The airmen were allocated one to each occupied cabin and, having each been issued with sleeping bags, our sleeping quarters were on the decks between the ratings' bunks. Within minutes I was known as 'Lofty' because of my being over 6ft tall, and so it remained until we left the craft at Halifax, Nova Scotia. The large naval mess deck was made available to the airmen to use with the ship's company both for meals and recreation. A far better arrangement than that on the *Royal Ulsterman*, where we had queued on the windswept deck in the open air.

As soon as the transfer was complete, our new home was released from the mooring buoy and with increasing speed headed for the open sea, soon to rendezvous with a battle cruiser named HMS *Resolution* and four accompanying destroyers. We rather felt that the destroyer screen was for the protection of the cruiser more than for us. For the next few days the convoy took a route across the North Atlantic, with the vessels heading into quite heavy seas. The cruiser certainly produced clouds of dense spray each time it butted into a wave, despite having the forward heavy gun turrets turned to either side on occasions. The biplane fitted with floats and mounted on a catapult towards the rear of the cruiser appeared to be unaffected by being in an exposed position.

The four destroyers kept station some 2 to 3 miles away day and night and sometimes the only indication that they were active was the thump of depth charges being dropped. Now and then a few airmen were required to carry out duties, but the number of available men far exceeded the jobs to be done. On several evenings off-duty sailors and airmen would gather together to enjoy the naval version of Bingo, which produced prizes far greater than was usual on the mess deck. Eventually, one fine morning a coastline appeared on the horizon ahead of us. At this point the *Derbyshire* increased speed and drew ahead of the other five warships, which turned away from our course and disappeared to the south on their way to Boston for repairs. In the meantime, we entered the waters of Halifax harbour, passed through the boom normally stretched across the entrance when there was no river traffic and moored alongside the dock. It was during the waiting time before disembarking that I was given a rocket by a naval lieutenant for taking photographs as a record of our arrival. Fortunately I was able to talk him out of confiscating my film. It would have been a considerable loss for I had been busy with the camera for some days.

The train waiting for us on nearby dockside tracks was headed by a monster steam engine and transfer across from the *Derbyshire* was speedily achieved, accompanied with shouts of 'All the best Lofty' from my cabin hosts standing on one of the upper decks. By this time it was 17 April.

Typically the Canadian railway passenger coaches were in Pullman style, being laid out with tables and bench seats for four travellers to each position. Meals appeared from a kitchen coach somewhere in the length of the train. Later in the evening the sleeping arrangements were made clear by a coach attendant. Tables and seats soon became beds and dropdown bunks from the coach roof screened by curtains provided the additional sleeping quarters. The airmen travelled in this fashion while the train took a wide sweep through New Brunswick until we reached Montreal and Toronto thereafter, some two days after leaving Halifax.

Frequent stops were convenient, allowing small purchases to be made from stores close to the station. Departure was signalled by a long-drawn-out hoot on the train horn, causing many stragglers to make a dash back. Long stretches of the railway line were single track, with double-track passing places where the train would puff and hiss while waiting for the oncoming train to thunder past. Many country roads were crossed by the line and the approach to these was accompanied by the mournful howl of the horn echoing across the countryside, especially at night in the manner familiar to followers of western films. Snow and ice at the most northerly stops gave way to improving temperatures and the last stage of the railway journey found us heading further west through Ontario on a brilliant morning, leaving Toronto far behind. No longer did we have the kitchen coach with us; breakfast that morning was in the restaurant coach, with bright white tablecloths, brilliant glass-ware and shiny cutlery, a most pleasant introduction to Ontario. Various groups of airmen had left the train for other destinations during the last two days and now some forty of us were destined for an airfield named Port Albert.

In the early afternoon the train ran into a station and town called Goderich. It stood on an elevated plateau overlooking the eastern shore of Lake Huron. Once there it was back to reality, humping kitbags and possessions into transport and generally being pressed to get a move on by a flight sergeant. Nothing had changed despite the many miles we had travelled from the UK, or by the Canadian accent. Soon all was loaded and the last stage of the journey commenced. It was off down a steep hill to the river level, across the steel-framed bridge and up to the high ground on the north side of the canyon. Once on open, level country-side good progress was made on the tarmac road running roughly parallel to the lake edge. After some miles that surface ran out and changed to a stony, sandy earth track. This was in fact the Blue Water Highway, which we were soon to realise dried out in the hot summer sun and each vehicle travelling along it left a swirling plume of dust trailing far behind. The convoy rumbled alongside a rough grass verge and wire fence past an isolated and lonely wayside snack bar on the left, braked and turned to the right through the guarded camp entrance and pulled up smartly in front of Hut 3. This was it. 'Everybody out.' The long journey from Aberystwyth was over. It was now 21 April 1941.

R.C.A.F. R. 96A
5M—8-40 (6373)
H.Q. 1062-3-79

AIR OBSERVERS NAVIGATION COURSE

Held at *N° 3 1. ANS*

From *21 APRIL 1941.* To *12 JULY 1941.*

SUBJECTS	MARKS		FLYING TIMES ON COURSE			
	Possible	Obtained	Type of a/c	Day	Night	
D.R.Nav	275	212	ANSON.	54:05	8:30	77
Compasses and Instruments	150	117				73
Meteorology	100	91				91
D.F. W/T	75	58				72½
Reconnaissance	100	86				86
Photography	100	96				96
Signals	100	90				90
Practical Work	500	380				76
MAPS AND CHARTS	100	91				91
QUALITIES AS N.C.O.	300.	210				70
TOTAL.	1800.	1431.				
	Total Marks obtained %	79.5%		TOTAL	54:05	8:30.

Remarks:— Passed
~~Failed~~

.... Instructor

NAVIGATION COURSE RESULTS.

Air observer navigation course results.

Chapter 2

New Faces, New Places

The arrival at Port Albert had been rapid and it was not until we stepped off the transport that I could cast a swift glance around to get an impression of our new surroundings. First impressions are important: three large hangars with the noise of an aero engine echoing from the tarmac on the far side; blocks of buildings looking solid and permanent, others mainly of timber; large open plots of land covered with mown grass, perhaps waiting to be built upon, and the timber domestic quarters where we were standing now, all looking remarkably like any other newly constructed airfield back at home. The familiarity was reassuring.

Lists of names were produced; the forty airmen were divided into two groups of twenty. The buildings were in plan form, built like a letter H: two barrack rooms with the service unit of toilets and showers sandwiched in between. Our companion group were Course 9 and my own group Course 10. Two-tier steel bunks lined the walls of the wooden hut and, having found a suitable spot, John King and I tossed a coin for choice of top or bottom bunk; he won and chose that on top so I had the bottom one. It was an amicable arrangement and remained so until we left Port Albert.

Before moving our kit into the living quarters our welcome to the camp had been punctuated by an outstretched arm and finger with: 'That building is station headquarters, that one is the instruction block and that one is the airmen's mess. Don't be late in the morning.' Sure enough, next morning there was no hanging about. It was on parade, a quick march to the instruction block and in the classroom 8 o'clock sharp. Introductions were brief. The course instructors were Flying Officer Coupland, Royal Canadian Air Force, and Flying Officer Jennings, Royal

Air Force. It was too early to make any judgement, that could come later. For now it was 'Right let us get on with it' and so we did.

'Here are your navigation watches. Sign for them on the form – we want them back before you leave here – and wind them up at the same time each day. I will give you a time check each morning; take a note regularly of how much your watch gains or loses in twenty-four hours, and only reset it if the correction becomes too large for the job you are doing. You are going to be navigators, time in the air is critical. Your watch is going to be your most important friend and aid.' Thus began a lifetime compulsion for being on time.

Seven days later came the day that had been in the forefront of our thoughts for many a long month. John King and I had teamed up to be together for all of the flying exercises and in the early afternoon of 28 April we hurried out in company with the other members of the course to the line of Anson aircraft drawn up on the tarmac. This was what had so far been our dream: our first flight. With the arrival of the new in-trepid airmen the pilot said, 'Hop in.' Our enthusiasm knew no bounds as John and I joined the pilot and wireless operator as instructed. The plan for each flight was that one trainee would act as first navigator with a set of exercises to complete, and the other of the pair would be occupied with supplementary duties. On the following flight the same exercises would be repeated but our roles would be reversed, so that each trainee received the same and equal instruction and experience.

Sitting next to the pilot I found that my main function was going to need a fair amount of effort. In quick time I was instructed on how to wind up the undercarriage and to change the sequence of the fuel tanks during flight, as I was sitting nearest to those controls. Under some mysterious hand the two engines in turn coughed into life, the propellers spun ever faster and we were rumbling across the tarmac towards the end of the runway. We surged down that long strip of concrete and the aircraft just floated off and I was being urged to wind up the undercar-riage. It was stiff. I had to put my strength and energy into the job. Having completed the required number of turns on the handle and breathing heavily, I noticed a smile on the pilot's face. I would try to avoid Anson U3 another time.

Where was the aerodrome? It had disappeared. Where were we? I was lost already. I looked frantically all round until the pilot pointed straight down. A breath of relief, it was directly below us under the wing. How did it get there? We were out over the lake a minute ago. Then a course was set and for the next two hours, while the pilot knew the route intimately – which was just as well – I flapped around trying to match conventional signs on the map with actual features on the ground. What I hadn't realised was the speed at which we travelled forward along the track on the ground so that my map reading progressed forward in a succession of jumps. However, by the time the aircraft started the third course back to base I was improving fast. Soon afterwards the aircraft was orbiting the airfield to make a landing, with the pilot making signs for me to wind down the undercarriage. With the end of the runway fast approaching I had to complete the job before the aircraft could touch down; with the weight of the landing gear in my favour it was slightly less difficult than my first encounter with it. Finished, with just a minute to spare. It was a day always to be remembered.

From this time forward, course lectures and other ground activities were punctuated with flying every two or three days. The layout of the 31 Air Navigation School (ANS) with its triangle of runways, line of hangars and mass of buildings laid out in straight lines close behind became a frequent and welcome sight, with the shore of Lake Huron just beyond, during the closing stages of yet another flight exercise. The lake played not only a significant part in the air exercises but also was a popular source for relaxation. Straight across the Blue Water Highway from the camp main entrance was a well-worn track through the fields to the lake edge. The wide shore backed by pine trees was ideal for swimming during the heat of the summer months in off-duty times.

Navigation and map reading became second nature, as did much of the supplementary duties of an observer, including signals and radio, meteorology, photography and the like. A great deal of effort and determination was expended in achieving the high standard results required by the course commanders.

All of the flying was done during daylight until early in July when take-off was timed in the late hours. This was a new experience, tearing down the flarepath with the lights streaming past on both sides and climbing

into a dark sky. Being a farming area lights in southern Ontario were well
scattered except in towns, which appeared as bright pools in the con-
trasting blackness. Fortunately these became recognisable in their relationship to form patterns in the way that is so with the stars. Flying over
some comparatively unlighted areas did bring to mind that when we
got back to the UK that would be normal, with the blackout to contend
with over the whole of the European area of conflict.

The course came to a conclusion later in July and exams were over. Results
were posted. From the expression on everyone's face they were reasonably
happy. I know I was. Now for seven days' leave. This was not the first
opportunity of leisure to occur, for most weekends had a good propor-
tion of free time. The nearest town, Goderich, was not too convenient to
visit, but OK for the occasional restaurant meal. So expeditions there
were not frequent, although there was an irregular bus service along
the dusty Blue Water Highway. There was an upside to this restriction
in that our expenditure was under control. Our leading aircraftmen
pay was also supplemented with flying pay, the daily rate amounting to
two and a quarter Canadian dollars. At that time I suppose the sterling
equivalent was about ten shillings and sixpence per day, the pound being
worth twenty shillings. Thus a comfortable sum accrued for the more
distant visits such as Toronto, which was some 140 miles away.

The first off-camp visit of the Port Albert posting occurred on the
second weekend with a block invitation from the residents of Stratford,
a medium-size town south-east of Goderich, having a strong association
with Stratford-upon-Avon in England. This was our first experience of
Canadian hospitality, which proved to be very welcoming indeed, and
was repeated wherever contact was made. On this particular occasion,
at the reception centre, the local residents were mingling with the
group of airmen and issuing invitations to stay the weekend. John King
and I were standing together when a young woman asked if we wished
to stay together; our answer of 'yes' prompted her to invite us to spend
the weekend with her parents and family. Soon we got into a large car and
were whisked away for a most enjoyable stay with them. Then it was back
on Sunday evening to Port Albert, ready for work on Monday morning.

At a later date, another Friday evening to Sunday evening visit, this time to Toronto, was fixed for Courses 9 and 10 by hiring a coach for all members of the two groups. Well not quite all, for four of the airmen had clubbed together and had bought an old Ford motor car of very early vintage and for a bet they were intending to drive to the city in the same time as the rest of us in the coach. After the day's course work was completed the car got away earlier than the coach and gained a nice number of miles in the lead. Once we got started, though, this was gradually reduced and we swept past with much banter and gestures, leaving them behind. However, the outcome of the wager was not yet resolved, for while pressing on in the Hamilton area the coach and its nearside back wheel parted company. The wheel, with much impetus, disappeared into the adjoining field; the coach gave us a rough ride for a few moments before coming to a halt. Down on the brake drum it wasn't going anywhere for the time being. Just under forty airmen lined the edge of the road, all with the same idea – to use their thumbs to hitch a lift.

There was a fair amount of traffic on this roadway, which indeed was a major route. The Canadian motoring population saw the situation in their headlights and pulled up, offering lifts without hesitation. The line of airmen began to diminish. Eventually a large motor car pulled up next to myself and two friends and the driver said 'Get in.'. The enquiries were brief: 'Where are you going?' … 'Where are you staying?' … 'Fine, I will take you there.' The driver of the car was adamant; this was something he wanted to do despite our protestations that it would make him very late getting home. The three of us – John King, another airman and myself – settled down, and as we glided along the Queen Elizabeth Highway not only did we have a great exchange of views and opinions but on entering the outskirts of Toronto we had a guided tour of the city right to the hotel entrance. Our thanks were accepted with great charm, accompanied by our 'chauffeur' saying that he had enjoyed the meeting greatly.

We never did resolve whether the quartet in the car or the coach party arrived first, but it did not matter as everyone reached there safely.

John King and I packed the two days with experiences of the vibrant city, a main recollection being the ability to travel on one tram journey of any length for a small basic fare, only paying again on changing to another individual route. So simple and effective.

The repaired coach appeared on time on Sunday evening for the journey back to Port Albert, only stopping en route to pick up two or three of the party who had been staying with family relatives. From the start it seemed that we had spent much time on relaxation, and certainly we made the most of the off-duty time. But, on the other hand, the twelve-week navigation course had demanded our full concentration and it was not long into the flying experience that the navigator's responsibilities as a member of an aircrew became abundantly clear.

So the seven days' promised leave was there to be exploited. Everybody seemed to have different ideas, as we could travel to all points of the compass. I decided to head for Toronto again, having put aside the idea of seeing the Rockies for it was virtually three days' train travel each way with only a brief period at Banff in Alberta. Coming off duty, having prepacked and with a quick change, I was soon on my way. After changing buses in Goderich I made my next stop at Clinton, alighting from the bus at a spot suitable to start the next stage only to find two airmen already there with the same purpose. They were Ron Batt and Crofton Selman from my own course, and it was obvious that they had got away more quickly than myself. They very kindly suggested that I travel with them. The bus service arrived, so we were on our way again, reaching the Ford Hotel in Toronto as a trio.

Early next morning Selman was off to keep an appointment with a contact who had been previously arranged by his father back in England. Ron Batt and I in the hotel awaited his return. He did not reappear but a telephone call came inviting us to a meeting at the Originals Club just off Younge Street and with instructions on how to get there. Within ten minutes the two of us stood knocking on the door of the club, to be invited in to join Selman and his host who explained that all the members were veterans of the 1914 to 1918 conflict with duty in one of the three major services. Mr Logan Selby, the member who we were meeting for the first time, told us that we were to be guests of the Ontario Motor League for our stay in Toronto. This was a staggering offer. The three of us had travelled to Toronto with no expectations in mind other than fending for ourselves from day to day. And now, at the beginning of the visit, we could only grin at each other and gratefully accept this most generous invitation. Soon we were at his home being introduced to Mary Selby, Logan's wife, and his daughter Jackie.

The following days were taken at a leisurely pace of meetings and greetings with other Canadian families and individuals, together with visits to many points of interest. A joy was a two-way trip across Lake Ontario to Niagara Falls to stay at the General Brock Hotel and also with a ride in the *Maid of the Mist* in the river close to the Horseshoe Falls, where we got somewhat wet. But at night in Toronto the mass of bright lights illuminating the cavernous city streets brought to mind the difference between life here with that back home, where the whole country was blacked out and experiencing the constant threat of air raids on the large cities, and rationing was a major topic of conversation.

The seven days soon swept by and it was time to return to Port Albert. Enjoyable as the visit had been, we were in Canada to do a job and the next stage was imminent. I was to see the Selby family again before returning to England. Logan Selby rejoined the Army with the rank of captain. We exchanged letters for many years after the war ended.

Back at the Navigation School the return to routine was welcome, our quarters in the domestic camp were the same, and there was a new intake of airmen starting the programme that we had completed. Courses 9 and 10 now embarked on the astro-navigation course of four weeks. The first few days were devoted to daytime flights using the sun sights for our introduction to the techniques covered by the lectures. Soon, however, night-time flights became dominant with the inherent problem of recognising the major stars in the constellations used in navigation. Time spent stargazing from the ground in evenings when off-duty paid dividends, especially when some parts of the sky were partially obscured by cloud and only part of a particular constellation was visible from the aircraft. On clear nights the sky looked immense from horizon to horizon – as indeed it was – and with the engines droning away the aircraft seemed to hang unmoving in space and the all-round darkness gave the sensation of an enveloping and smothering environment. A few months later, back in our home country, flying at night with no outside lights showing below, the darkness of a moonless night was emphasised, but strangely comforting, especially with there being the possibility of encountering a Luftwaffe intruder.

During those four weeks the techniques of turning the readings with the sextant of the heavenly bodies into positions on the chart and then to ground positions became clear, but the accuracy depended on the skill in using the sextant, allied with an accurate note of the time utilised in taking the sights that the instrument averaged out for the navigator. Unstable flying conditions were a constant hazard to getting a good result. Returning back to within a few miles of the starting point of an exercise was considered to be a fair outcome. At this early point in the training this did not happen every time.

Throughout my stay at Port Albert I had often thought of exploring the nearby coastline. On one of the last Saturdays there I resolved to walk the 12 miles into Goderich by that route. The lake edge was rimmed with a beach and a pine tree background with numerous small groups of wooden cottages used by families at weekends and holidays. The final stage of the path was interrupted by the river at the bottom of the canyon near the edge of town. The road bridge out of town was some way off, but I was walking along a single railway track that ran straight to the edge of the high ground and then bridged the gap with a wood-framed trestle structure typical of Canadian railway construction. There did not seem to be any activity at the other end so I took the first step on the wood sleepers and continued across. The drop to the river below was spectacular viewed though the gap between the timbers. To my good fortune no train appeared; if one had I am still not sure what action I would have taken for there was no protective railing on either side. The town was only a short distance away, so I had saved myself a very considerable detour. My information now is that the track was later abandoned and the bridge was adapted to provide a popular public walkway across the canyon.

The astro-navigation course came to an end with a flurry of night flights, putting the theory of the lecture room into practical usage. Once again it was time to pack all one's belongings and also to come to a decision on how much one could bear to throw away because there was no more baggage room. Air Ministry property just did not get discarded. The domestic quarters were left clean, with no indication left that you had spent four months of your life there. Not even an echo. We had gone.

Goderich town and its railway station disappeared rapidly into the hazy distance as the engine and several passenger coaches bombed their way down the track towards our next destination. August 1941 was drawing to a close – the last astro sight, the last aerial photograph and the last navigation flight from Port Albert had been taken and now we were off to a new experience. The route appeared to be international, for names such as Stratford, London and St Thomas marked the journey; the latter was where the railway terminated and the remaining few miles were in a lorry, the normal air force form of transport.

The new air base – No. 4 Bombing and Gunnery School – was located at Fingal, and again only a short distance from the edge of one of the Great Lakes. This was the third of the five Great Lakes that we had become associated with and this time it was Lake Erie. There are many European place names in south Ontario, but this one was rather strange. However, in this case it was a particularly appropriate name for an armaments establishment. Fingal or 'Fion na Gael' was a warrior son of Comhal and Morna of the kingdom of Moruen in north-west Scotland. After many battles he eventually resigned his spear and died in ad 283.

Soon the countryside opened out. A vast, flat featureless space appeared, which seemed to stretch to the horizon; it was an illusion, naturally, due to low hedges in the distance and nothing else of any height. The road ran alongside the perimeter of the airfield and our transport entered the entrance to the main working camp on its way to the domestic quarters. In so doing we passed a number of directional signs; one in particular caught my eye, which spelled out 'Attention Area'. I said to my neighbour, 'Did you see that?', but of course he hadn't. I thought that we were in for a few surprises on this camp for it was a Royal Canadian Air Force (RCAF) establishment, unlike Port Albert, which was RAF.

Early impressions that first evening provided little variation to our previous experience. Importantly, the food was to prove very good with many variations typical of the Canadian style of catering. Yet just one matter made an immediate impact because all water from the bore hole on site had a strong sulphur content and could only be used for showers, baths and washing. It did not require any imagination to realise the pungency of the water when hot. Fortunately drinking water was imported.

Shortly, some thirty airmen under training split up into almost two equal groups and settled down to the routine of the new course. We followed the previous requirement to take the practical exercises in pairs,

which suited Johnny King and myself for we had developed an easy working relationship.

On the morning of the first flight we were down at the departure area
earlier than necessary, just to get feel of a new type of aircraft. Standing
there with a touch of mist floating in the early light there was a long line
of single-engined low-winged planes with a transparent housing along
the top of the fuselage. The sight of the ensemble of Fairey Battles, with
the sunlight glinting along the edges of the wings and bodywork of the
silhouetted aircraft, was incredibly exciting, bringing back visions of the
old film *The Dawn Patrol*. But, new they were not, for they were the same
type as those that had been on RAF front-line strength years previously.
Even so, they had formed the first ten squadrons sent to France at the
beginning of September 1939 to form the Advanced Air Striking Force.

Once again, stepping out on to the tarmac was a critical moment; the
lectures, practical demonstrations and studies of the previous week were
to be put to the test. Most of the pilots serving here were from the United
States of America. F.O. Smith was the pilot taking Johnny and myself
into the sky today. He urged us to climb into the positions in the main
section of the fuselage and to get familiar with the layout inside. I was
to take the first set of attempts at the target, so John climbed up and took
over the air gunner's position; meanwhile, I was down on my knees on
the floor of the aircraft looking down through a large round opening
over which was perched the Mark 9 bombsight. There was just time to
set up the sight with the necessary instructions and data when the pilot
spoke through the voice pipe to say that he was starting up and was I
ready to go? 'Yes sir.' I did hope that I was.

The three-bladed propeller turned, the engine coughed and roared
and shook the plane, like a lion getting up after sleep. I could see the
tarmac speeding by through my observation hole; we were on our way.
I felt the tail swing and, then, the engine power and the noise all increased.
The runway rushed underneath and suddenly it was almost quiet as the
wheels left terra firma; the engine was on reduced power and the ride
was smooth, but all I could see was the view through the hole in the floor.
The ground was fast receding. The plane levelled out at the correct height
and at the required speed and I was informed that the exercise had
started. I looked out at the lake surface below – where the devil was that

target? Eventually, its triangular shape swam into view under the front end of the hole (bombing observation aperture) and I could start to give my directions to the pilot: 'Right, right, steady, steady, left, left, steady.' The target travelled along the guide lines on the bombsight until it was in the actual sights. 'Bomb gone.' It dropped into view and I watched it fall away; as it drew closer to the ground it appeared to race along the surface of the lake at an ever increasing rate until it splashed into the water not far from the target. Beginner's luck! The pilot swung the plane around on to a new course to try again, and again, until my six bombs were gone and it was time for John to take his turn.

We changed places and I took over in the air gunner's position and enjoyed the superb view of the countryside running down to the lake and across the water to the target, sitting on the surface about half a mile offshore. With all the practice bombs used up and the exercise completed, the pilot headed for base to repeat the task with two more trainees. John and I had already formed a good idea of our results but were keen to see if they had yet come through from the range-monitoring post by land line. They hadn't, of course, so we had to wait in eager anticipation.

This was the general run of each day, with at least one flight and some-times two, with training taking place at all heights from low level to 10,000ft. Strangely, the low-level work was the most troublesome, with the limited view forward through the hatch in the floor of the Fairey Battle to pick up the target, give adjustments to the pilot on the direction the aircraft was flying and get the bomb away before overflying the target. On an earlier high-level flight it was my job to make the decision that the particular approach to the target was going badly – the heading of the aircraft, combined with the wind and our closeness to the aiming point, ensured a lack of success. So I told the pilot that it was a 'dummy run'! He must have been having a bad day. The nose of the Battle dropped, speed built up, he pulled the control column back and we went up to the top of a loop. I was pinned to the floor by the G force, unable to move until he rolled off the top into level flight. With only the comment, 'Let us try again shall we', we did just that. I do not remember John King's comment on the manoeuvre for he was standing in an open cockpit. Fortunately he was strapped in.

I seem to remember that in 1942, when the American Eighth Air

Force entered the conflict in Europe, that their bombardiers promised us that they could drop a bomb into a pickle barrel from 10,000ft. Well, oddly enough a year earlier there was already at No. 4 B&G School at Fingal, a symbol of that saying in the form of 'The Pickle Barrel Club' to foster competition among the airmen under instruction. The sole requirement for membership was to make a direct hit on the bombing target from high level during an exercise. A creditable number of our course did so; those who succeeded were presented with a bronze membership badge in recognition of their achievement. I still have mine.

By the time the bombing course had entered its third week the gunnery training had started and it was at this stage that the previous service on ground defence at Bircham Newton showed its value, for those of us who had experienced those duties already had a good knowledge of the equipment and of firing the guns. The flights for the actual firing were a joy for it was from the open cockpit that the exercise took place. Standing in the open air with a vast space all around and the lake below on a beautiful late summer morning needed to be experienced to be fully appreciated, especially after the bombing practice, which required the participant to lie on the floor of the enclosed fuselage with very limited vision except downwards. Another Fairey Battle painted bright yellow with large diagonal black stripes would fly a long, straight flight path out over the lake towing a white drogue some considerable distance behind and the trainee gunner would blaze away with the machine gun mounted on a scarfe ring for support, hoping to achieve a large number of hits. When he had expended his ration of ammunition his companion would then replace him and carry out his own exercise using the same drogue, his ammunition being marked with red so that the two results could be separately counted after the drogue-towing aircraft had dropped it on to the airfield for examination.

A little relief from the constant instruction with bullets and bombs came my way with one or two others from the course, when we attended a research project being carried out at the hospital in London, Ontario, a town about an hour's drive away to the north of St Thomas, which was our nearest shopping centre. The project was an investigation into the reaction of aircrew to oxygen starvation when flying at very high levels. To simulate high flight four of us had to climb into a large decompression chamber accompanied by a doctor. We sat around a table and carried out arithmetic and other exercises as the air pressure was gradually reduced until the equivalent height to 10,000ft was reached, and as was usual practice in the RAF we then went on to oxygen. The air pressure continued to reduce until it was representative of 30,000ft. Mental exercise had continued, with little effect if any being seen. One at a time the airmen took off their oxygen masks, with their reactions being noted by the medical staff. Within two or so minutes all ability to perform exercises or tasks disappeared and only a few instinctive movements remained. After a few minutes the oxygen supply was returned to them and the change back to normal behaviour was observed. The remaining difficulty was convincing that person just how far out of this world he had been for those few minutes. After seeing the effect on the others we were persuaded of the effect and the dangers. To the individual on limited oxygen it was like being in 'happy time'; all one's cares seemed to disappear. There was, of course, the added incentive to attend the repeat sessions, for we had some free hours each time to enjoy the benefits of the entertainment of a large town, as well as being transported there without the charge of the fare.

Ahead of us another group composed entirely of New Zealand airmen completed their training programme. This was recognised with a passing-out parade, which coincided with a visit by their own prime minister, Peter Fraser, who made the presentation of their brevets. The whole of the training wing turned out in best blue to attend and mark such an event. It was important to recognise the successful completion of many months of work so far from home.

And now it was 29 September 1941; this was our last day at Fingal. Was it only yesterday that John and I had hitched a lift back to camp with a young man not even our own age yet. On our way back he had drawn my attention to his flying log book lying on the seat of the car. As he obviously intended, I picked it up to see how many hours' flying he had acquired. I nearly fell off the seat and passed the document to John, exclaiming: '600?' He nodded. I thought, what have we been doing these last six months? 'Hours?' I queried. 'Oh no,' he said, 'minutes.' What could one say but 'Very good.' Our rather meagre 130 hours began to look better.

Bags and practically all one's possessions were now packed and there was
the air of 'going away', as indeed we were, this very afternoon. The only
sign of consistent occupation was the best blue tunic complete with
new sergeant stripes on the sleeves and a bright new observer's brevet
on the left-hand chest hanging over each bed head. 'Everybody on parade'
came the call and this was the last time to carry out the order as a leading aircraftman. No hanging back on this occasion. Smart as new paint
the squad marched through the attention area on to the parade ground
and into the open square left for us by other units of airmen and invited
guests. Sixteen of us stood in line; the afternoon had suddenly fallen
quiet, even the hot breeze had seemed to die. Then one by one names were
called. Each man received his observer's brevet from an army general. It
was a significant moment in an RAF career to be remembered.

The barrack room echoed with loud voices and activity as the old uniforms with LAC ranking were packed away, to be brought up to date at
some time in the future. The newly promoted sergeants gathered their
belongings, ready to pile them into the motor vehicle waiting outside.
Nothing was left behind – every scrap of personal gear had gone, the
beds were bare metal frames; whoever took over the accommodation
would draw replacement bedding from the stores. As at Port Albert, it
was as if we had never been there. Travel warrants, meal tickets where
required, money, leave passes with instructions to be at No. 1Y Depot,
Halifax, Nova Scotia, on 3 October – all these were safely tucked into
tunic pockets. Just the time and direction one took to get to the new
depot was our own responsibility.

For myself, Toronto was my first stop, with the initial night at the Royal
York Hotel. This was followed by my goodbyes to the Selby family, with
promises on both sides to keep in touch. We did so for many years.
Then it was on to Montreal, meeting up on the train with one of my companions from the course. Both of us tried to get into the YMCA, but it
was full up. Seeing a notice, 'Rooms to let', we went up some stairs between
two shops. The room and beds looked clean so we decided to stay for
two nights, even though we came away with some doubts about the other
occupants upstairs. After that it was off to the station to book ourselves
on to a train, with a day room with two bunks. The train thundered on
through daylight and night-time hours towards Halifax, with the two

of us eating and sleeping in reasonable comfort. The room was worth the extra cost. En route the woods from the window were full of red and yellow colours; the 'Fall' was in full swing.

At Halifax, 'Y' Depot, dozens of new aircrew sergeants were booking in, with everyone heading for the UK. All were given sleeping quarters, their names already recorded; one was checked in as on time. The hours hung rather heavily and two days passed. Finally lists were put up on the noticeboard; your name and number were there, as were those of your friends from Fingal, and a time and date to be ready was indicated. As the appointed time arrived, transport took those listed, with all their kit-bags, down to the docks where a very large ship, the *Andes*, waited along-side the quay.

The side of the ship stretched upward as if it was a gigantic wall; well I suppose that it was. Sloping gangways reached from the dockside to holes in the wall and servicemen were struggling up these wood slopes with their kit and disappearing into the openings. I joined my fellow travellers and once inside followed the instructions on the berthing card: 'Up several levels to Deck F and seek out berth No.1'. The quarters were rather cramped but level with one of the promenade decks; it was fine. All my worldly goods were stored in four kitbags. I retained one packed for the voyage and the other three went down into the hold to be retrieved before disembarking.

Cheers and the sounds of departure drew me outside and, indeed, the space between the hull and the quay had widened and the gangways were parked on the quayside. Servicemen lined the side rails of the decks, three and four deep, and some of them had climbed on to the lifeboats and up the ladder attached to the rear mast to get a good view of the leave-taking and also to see and wave to onlookers ashore. The *Andes* was not the only vessel to depart; three other large ships were heading in line ahead towards the open sea. Once through the boom across the harbour mouth speed was gradually increased, and the deck began to heave gently underfoot. With a little mist softening the horizon, the ships of the convoy adopted their appointed steaming positions. The port of Halifax disappeared behind us, leaving a feeling, once again, of leaping into the unknown.

The Commanding Officer and Officers
wish you all a Happy Christmas.

ROYAL AIR FORCE, LICHFIELD.

Christmas Dinner, 1941.

MENU.

OX TAIL SOUP.

ROAST TURKEY.

ROAST PORK AND APPLE SAUCE.

BOILED GAMMON.

ROAST POTATOES.   BRUSSELS SPROUTS.

———

CHRISTMAS PUDDING.   BRANDY SAUCE.

MINCE PIES.

———

ALES.   MINERALS.

LOMAX, PRINTER, LICHFIELD.

RAF Lichfield Christmas dinner menu 1941.

Chapter 3

The Men from Oz

One grey misty day was followed by another, only to be relieved by a few hours of bright sunshine and limitless visibility. One morning, however, the noisy wash of the ocean was suddenly broken by the roar of aircraft engines. Two twin-engined planes swept over the *Andes* at little more than masthead height. I still have the feeling that they were North American Mitchells but cannot be sure. We had not heard them coming as we were standing on the deck away from the side of their approach. Two or three low-level runs through the convoy and they were away out of sight in a few seconds. Who they were and where they had come from was never revealed, but it lifted our spirits considerably. Nor were we any the wiser as to where we were either, other than somewhere in the North Atlantic. What we could do was admire the standard of the air navigation of these aircraft, resulting in the interception at a remote location in the vast space of the ocean. During training, one or two exercises had been flown to introduce the concept to us, but it was very tricky with all participants on the move.

Coming out on deck one morning I became aware that we were steaming along a coastline, turning around, and retracing our route, only for the *Andes* to turn again on to our original course. Some airmen were up earlier than me and were quite happy to broadcast their knowledge. The coast was that of North Wales and Anglesey and as the ship was now continuing ahead it soon entered the Mersey and came to a halt in midstream opposite the Royal Liver Building. It was now only a matter of time before we were to disembark.

Thinking back over the two crossings that had gone so well I was reminded not only of the two aircrews that found the convoy, but also of the sight of one of the ships, in addition to the *Resolution*, that had been fitted with a catapult on which had been mounted a Spitfire. Apparently this was to be launched for defence in the event of an air attack. Imagine the stress on the fighter pilot constantly at sea waiting for the call to take off, knowing that at the end of the sortie, all being well – and with the standard landing gear – he had to ditch in mid-ocean and hope to successfully escape from the cockpit and be picked up from the water. A daunting prospect indeed. I still wonder if the aircraft was ever put into use.

Then it was off the *Andes*, with feet on steady ground again – and home ground too – before boarding the train with all our kit. Bournemouth here we come! One image of that journey remains with me – how very green was the English countryside. The Canada that we left behind was all browns, ochres and reds.

Well how nice it was to be by the seaside, at least it would be after a good night's sleep. This came after we struggled into Byng Mansions in Boscombe with all those damn kitbags. The Mansions were not so impressive as their name; every piece of furniture had been removed and replaced with primitive metal-framed beds, lockers and an occasional wood chair. The bare floorboards, lit by an unshaded single electric light bulb per room, did nothing to improve the sombre surroundings. Morning, sunshine, hot water, breakfast. Wasn't it great to be back?

The reception centre was spread around central Bournemouth, close to the Winter Gardens and nearby buildings. They knew you were here, you were on the list. There were instructions to 'Go to this address, it's the medical centre.' Then it was: 'Morning Sergeant. What is your night vision like?' 'OK I guess sir.' 'Well we will find out for sure, sit there'. The result was entered into my flying log book and read as 'Night Vision Test B'Mth. 25/10/41. Above average.'

Next came lunch in the sergeants' mess. Soon I was not wanted any more today, and was told to report back tomorrow. The rest of the day was now my own, a good opportunity to look around the town and meet a couple of friends. We wandered into the shopping area. 'Look there, Bobby's'; it was a well-known department store. It was now afternoon teatime, so the three of us decided to investigate. 'Yes, sir, the tearoom is upstairs. … Yes there is always a table free for the air force.' So it was tea, scones and jam for three please.

Three grey-haired ladies in black gowns appeared and mounted the rostrum where there was a piano; one carried a violin, another had a cello and the third sat down at the piano. After a little preparation, Ivor Novello's music floated across the tearoom to the appreciation of their devotees.

That evening I met Elizabeth, and my social life took a step forward and improved.

Two days later the duty day was still less than fully occupied, but the word 'leave' was the popular topic in conversation now. Soon it became a substantial promise of documents to be distributed 'tomorrow'. This left ample time to pack just what one needed for the period away, sort out the train timetable, enjoy the evening and make arrangements for my return. The admin staff came up trumps. Pay was now in our pockets, together with leave passes and travel warrants. Dressed in 'best blue' the contingent from Port Albert were off to all parts of the country. I made it home for my twenty-second birthday on 1 November 1941. I had been on duty overnight at Bridgnorth for my twenty-first.

As always, seven days' leave passed quickly and it was back to Bournemouth transit camp and that room in Byng Mansions. It still looked miserable, and there was yet no posting waiting for me. There were so many aircrew from the Empire Air Training Scheme waiting to start their next stage in this country that patience was needed.

The previous routine continued, with some additional lectures and events to keep us occupied. One day was devoted to a major parade of service personnel for a formal visit by King George VI and the Queen. He was not as big a man as I had imagined, although he had served in the Royal Navy and the Royal Air Force for he displayed pilot wings on his uniform, but an excess of make-up did him no favours. Good for the press photographers no doubt.

As each day went by, the November weather continued to be unusually warm and pleasant. The promenade in the town was well used by many people both in and out of uniform, especially in the part between the pier by the pavilion and that at Boscombe. What on earth did we need all that barbed wire on the beach for? The evenings were pleasant too, plenty of entertainment of all sorts. Then Elizabeth announced that she would be going on night duty at the hospital from the following week; this would upset our evening plans and arrangements. As if a premonitory signal had been given, the next day postings were put up. Oh yes! My name was there too, with others of the same group, but I did not see anyone else going to the same destination as I was. RAF Lichfield, where on earth was that? It didn't take long to find out, for it was in Staffordshire to the north of Birmingham.

Then it was two days before we were off. Time to vacate that room at Byng Mansions in Boscombe at last. At the station we said our final goodbyes, with promises to write, before I took the morning train. Some time later the train ran into Lichfield Trent Valley station. Surrounded by my kit I took a quick look round: red-brick Victorian station buildings and a high-level platform with a line running across the main route, a local line I supposed. Ah yes! There was the station yard, cars and vehicles, and people stepping off the platform and out through that gate. The crowd diminished fast; they all knew where they are going. Who was left? I saw a group of a dozen or fifteen officers and sergeants, the majority dressed in dark blue – obviously Royal Australian Air Force – with the remainder in RAF colours to match my own. I joined the group. It appeared that we all had the same destination. Introductions were brief and incomplete as an air force vehicle pulled into the yard to collect us. Luggage was crammed in, aircrew much the same. The driver took us up the station approach, turned right on to the Burton Road across the bridge and we were on our way.

Our understanding was that we would not be going to the main Lichfield camp, which was quickly passed, but to a satellite establishment for the next two or three weeks. On the outskirts of Burton upon Trent we turned off on to a minor road and then on to an access leading to a severe-looking country house. As we came to a halt by a group of buildings my eyes told me this set-up was a stable yard. The thought crossed my mind as to whether parking here was significant. It turned out to be the accommodation for the sergeants, for we were directed to get our kit inside. The interior was clean, very clean, with not a horse in sight, nor even the smell of horses, which was remarkable. Instead, each of the stalls was fitted out to take three men, the general command being to sort ourselves out and somebody would be round to explain where the sergeants' mess was, meal times, and other important matters and details. I wandered into one of the stalls, to be followed by two Aussie pilots. 'OK if we join you? I'm Don and this is Ralph.' 'Yes, sure, I'm Gordon.' It was as easy as that.

It took our source of information some time to answer the many questions shot at him, but one answer was received with mixed feelings. In response to the question of 'Where are we?' it appeared that we were at a place known as King's Standing, some 4.5 to 5 miles outside Burton upon Trent to the east, where even the air was supposed to be intoxicating. But there was no public transport to take us to that town. Much to everyone's surprise some days elapsed before we found out that there was an airfield named Tatenhill just across the road to the front of the country house. There had so far been no sound of aircraft taking off or landing; perhaps it was unmanned. That was to be resolved much later.

The period that followed was similar to that at previous training establishments. It was like being back at school again, except that when the pilots and navigators combined there were still only fourteen of us in total: nine pilots and five navigator/observers. There was one pilot missing from the group at this stage. The main intention of the staff was to encourage the group to crew up together into units of two pilots and one navigator. The remaining crewmembers were to be found when we transferred to the main camp. There was much discussion with the pilots having to sort themselves out. Three pilots were officers, the remainder being sergeants. For a day or two the navigators held back to assess how the pairs of pilots reacted with each other. In fact, it was all rather academic as far as I was concerned, having already quite happily joined up with my two room companions Don Jennings and Ralph Longmuir.

On the middle Saturday of our stay at King's Standing I decided that I may not have another chance to visit Burton upon Trent again for quite some time, so I set off to walk the few miles there, it being a fine morning; nobody else followed my example. There was no doubt that I had arrived for the smell of brewing on the breeze was quite strong. I do recall looking for and finding a bookshop, the main object of my visit; I think it was W.H. Smith. I have no strong recollection whatsoever of how I got back to the country house and the stable block and, before anybody makes the suggestion, I did not stop in any of the taverns to sample the local brew. Probably I returned along the same route as my outward journey. The day came for our transfer to Lichfield airfield, uneventful in itself, but there was a significant and welcome change to our living quarters and also an awareness that we would recommence flying. That important event occurred on 16 December 1941.

Pilots and navigators separated to pursue their particular requirements, the pilots to convert on to the Wellington 1c, and the navigators on to Avro Ansons, again to experience flying conditions in the British Isles. The first flight was in the morning in daylight and the second during the night of the same day. Back in the air again – three months since my last flight at Fingal in southern Ontario – and what a difference in flying conditions! The bright sunlight and almost limitless visibility of summer in Canada had been replaced by a grey, misty day. This was what was to be expected now, best get used to it. We flew out over the coast at Rhyl, with no more landmarks below, just sea. A few courses across the water, with a quick glimpse of the Isle of Man, and it was eventually back to Rhyl on the way home. The question was did we make the correct landfall on the mainland coast? In the event it was not bad at all, just under the starboard wingtip, and so we set a course for base at Fradley. We were down on the runway after three and a half hours.

Although that was not too difficult, what about tonight? This would be another proposition altogether, for it would be the first time in 'blackout' wartime conditions. By the time darkness fell, the preparations for the night flight were complete, with the flight plan worked up using the direction of each track to be flown, the cruising airspeed of the aircraft, and the wind speed and direction from the forecast supplied by the Met. Office. The plotting chart was drawn up with the route ready to work on. The engines of the Anson roared into life and the flare path set out before us began to speed past the observation windows on each side; in seconds it was left behind and the pilot, Squadron Leader Davies, took us up into the blackness.

It was so dark I couldn't see a damn thing, but I passed the first course to be flown to the pilot. But hang on a minute, there was the flare path coming up ahead down there. We were right on top of the airfield now;

I logged the time and checked that the pilot was on the course that I gave him. I turned the light over the navigation table down; could anything be seen? Yes there was a faint blue light from some of the towns, and some aerodromes were flashing an identification signal of two letters. It was not so dark now, my eyes were getting used to the low light levels. There was a river gleaming in the starlight, so I tried to get a visual position. Were we on track? The radio operator got a couple of bearings, and every piece of information and the time was logged and plotted on the chart. We were slightly off track – the wind was lighter than forecast – so it was necessary to establish new wind direction and speed before projecting the position forward, calculating the new course for five minutes ahead and revising the estimated time of arrival at the next turning point. I notified the pilot of the change in direction for him to alter course to be on time.

And so the attention continued, until that satisfying moment when you saw the flare path of your home base appear up front, to be followed by the screech of the main landing gear touching down and you could make the final entry in the log of the time and the word 'Landed'. This was basic navigation; it was essential to keep the log and chart up to date all the time, to check all calculations and constantly gather positional information. You had to watch the clock. There was no room for mistakes. In a very short time you got the message loud and clear. This was serious stuff. The rest of the crew depended on you absolutely to get them there and back safely.

Day and night flying continued on a daily basis, sometimes twice in every twenty-four hours. Even landing away at RAF Silloth well after midnight, which gave us a few early morning hours of sleep in the armchairs in the mess, followed by breakfast and then another daylight return to 27 Operational Training Unit (OTU), Lichfield.

Christmas Day arrived. No flying, but a most enjoyable tradition in which the officers and senior NCOs acted as waiters and served Christmas lunch to all the airmen and WAAFs on the camp. For a short time a massive light-hearted gathering of perhaps up to a thousand or more people held in the airmens' mess hall made the most of a unique situation. In with the Christmas mail I received a letter from John Wilkin, who had been left behind at ITW in Aberystwyth. His health problem had been resolved and he was now taking his navigation course at the University of Miami in the United States. The major difference was that at Miami on practical exercises the aircraft used were large flying boats of the style used by Pan Am, with a considerable capacity for passengers. This space was used for groups of trainees, with one being selected to be the prime navigator responsible for carrying out the exercise and the remainder plotting the result. Therefore you had a while to wait for your turn as Nav 1. On the RAF system of training in Canada, such experience was gained in pairs, the lead being taken on alternate flights.

The festivities being over, the regular flying recommenced both day and night, very often with the same pilots several times running, with Flying Officer Newbury and Sergeant Treharne joining the squadron leader. On one night flight my confidence received a savage but temporary blow. The route had taken us to the east before altering course to fly up through Lincolnshire and Yorkshire. As was usual the wireless operator supplied me with a couple of radio bearings that I plotted on my chart, adjusting the first to coincide with the time of the second to give me a fix. To my horror it gave our position as out over the North Sea, but we were supposed to be over land inside the east coast. It was cloudy below, no point in taking a look down. The wind had been checked, it could not have altered so much, and all my other work checked out. The wireless operator couldn't get more bearings for he was having his own problems. I had to do something, so after studying the chart again I decided that they were rogue bearings and that I should rely on my own efforts. We flew on, turned on to another course on DR (Deduced Reckoning) on my calculated time, and to my relief eventually ran over broken cloud to reveal expected landmarks, at which point my anxieties began to drop away. It was a salutary lesson and was a boost to my confidence in my own work.

It was 17 January 1942 and change was in the air. Morning parade was over and pilots and navigators were down in the 'B' flight crew room. The flying in Ansons was in the past for Vickers Wellingtons were parked in the dispersals. Don Jennings and Ralph Longmuir were detailed off to fly circuits and bumps and I went along, for this was to be the first time flying together as a crew. As this was to be local flying I climbed into the rear turret and we were airborne, with a screened pilot with us supervising up front. I found flying with my back to the direction of flight rather a strange experience. You had to be sharp on map reading to identify the landmark before it disappeared from you. Having gone halfway round the flight circuit Don turned into the approach to the runway, the aircraft sank down and soon the screech of the tyres on the runway was heard; we slowed to taxying speed and ran round the perimeter track to halt near the control tower, briefly. Then it was off again to repeat the performance, including the short stop on the apron near control afterwards. But what on earth was the instructor doing waiting out on the tarmac?. Then it became obvious that Don had just flown solo in a Wellington. Congratulations were made all round.

For the subsequent repetition I changed my position to the front turret. To enter the turret a bulkhead door had to be unlocked, and after taking up the position it was locked back in place again. Facing the direction of flight was immediately familiar. However, when approaching the start of the runway to land I felt that it was just under my toes as the aircraft started to descend; it was quite a steep approach and the sensation was different from that while sitting at the rear. It was good to get the feel of flying in a front-line-type aircraft and a step forward from the Avro Anson. Even so, I did recall that there had been a squadron of Ansons operating out of RAF Bircham Newton during the period when we were there occupied on ground defence.

The crewing up started to come together, and I had been lucky in my original arrangement. Since arriving at the main camp at Fradley, Don Jennings and I had shared our two-bed accommodation. Ralph was close by. Now we gathered in young Bill Godfrey from Perth in Western Australia as rear gunner and Ted Willey as wireless operator. The remaining position in the nose turret was filled by Ralph Webb.

Daylight cross-country flights dominated, with other activities such as various photographic tasks and dropping practice bombs at the range at Cannock Chase; these latter events fell upon me, as these had been covered during the time spent in Canada. Flight times lengthened, occasionally to over five hours.

Following the Christmas break and when duties allowed, which was quite often, Don and I would walk into Lichfield town in the late afternoon. By the second visit we had sorted out the best place for tea. This proved to be the Tudor cafe, situated in an old half-timbered building in Blore Street. The atmosphere was in keeping with the building, the proprietors were pleasant and welcoming, the food was good and the young ladies waiting at table – such as Doreen, who would often serve us – were very attractive. The two of us became regulars and very well known there. Even after a span of sixty-five years the Tudor cafe is still there and in business. Much remains the same, but the waitresses there now are of a more mature age. I haven't been in there for tea for quite a long time now; for me it has lost some of its former attraction somehow. Doreen used to be quite a charmer all those years ago.

The winter was cold, icy cold, so much so that the large pond in the open ground between the perimeter track and the Burton Road froze over so that ice skating was safe. Heavy snow covered the airfield and the planes parked in the open gave the maintenance crews of all trades great problems in trying to keep them serviceable. Sweeping the top surface of the wings was not without its dangers. I saw one airman slip on the ice on the wing of a Wimpy and fall to the ground, his fellow riggers rushing to help. It was a fall of quite a height on to concrete hard ground, causing injury. Visibility at Fradley also suffered from north-westerly winds, which brought smoke and industrial fumes down from Liverpool to cause varying foggy conditions over a wide area. Not a good winter by any standard.

As we progressed through February weather conditions improved, and on the 26th of the month Don took us up in the early afternoon, with Ralph as second pilot, on local flying to the bombing range. Following wheels-up I let one of the crew into the front turret, securing the bulkhead door behind him. The rest of us were then in our flying positions, ready to set course over the centre of the airfield. Within minutes, over the outskirts of Lichfield, Don called that he was having trouble with the starboard engine, and although he tried to increase its power there was little response. At this point we would normally be climbing for height and this was not happening. The decision was made to return to base, which meant taking a route to approach the end of the runway. The next call was that the engine was failing and even with the other one on full power we could not maintain height.

This was now serious, and there were still a scattering of houses below. The airfield could be seen away to port. It was a matter now of having enough height to reach it. I nipped down to the nose of the Wimpy, released the bulkhead and let the front occupant up into the fuselage behind the two pilots, relocked the bulkhead and then joined him. Through the side windows of the aircraft I saw the upper roof of the Trent Valley railway station flash past our wingtip almost at our level. The main-line railway track passed underneath.

We were not going to make the airfield.

The Wellington hit a sloping meadow nose first, skidding along. The tail slammed down and we came to an abrupt halt. The quietness was deafening. Then, a faint creaking as the airframe settled and a sound of dripping, but it couldn't be water. I was still standing up, frenziedly cling-ing on with my arms wrapped around a metal post, which is what had saved me from being thrown into the nose of the aircraft when we hit the ground. Where were the others? I couldn't see, there was smoke every-where, but I knew I must get out. The astrodome was just above my head, held in position by two catches; it was only necessary to undo one catch and it would pivot down on the opposite side. One had to press two lugs together and that side would be freed. It appeared to be jammed shut. I struggled to release the catch but it wouldn't move. Suddenly the lugs slid together and the dome swung down. I could poke my head out into the air. Somehow my shoulders followed and I slid down the side of the fuselage head first on to the port wing and over the trailing edge to the ground.

Don was lying on the ground quite some yards away from the front of the aircraft. 'How did you get there Don?'

'Walked straight out the front.'

'Are you all right?'

'There is something wrong with my leg.'

'OK, hang on.' I left him there for a minute while I went to check on the others. The front turret had broken off and rolled halfway across the field. The impact had been fierce. Thank heaven there was nobody left in it. But petrol was dripping on to the starboard engine and it was burning. Off to the tail end; here was potential tragedy. Bill Godfrey was unconscious and trapped in the rear turret. Fortunately a small gang of workmen from the nearby railway came running up, carrying a variety of tools. They took in the gravity of the situation when told that there was a fire brewing in one of the engines. Ted Willey and I grabbed a shovel each, ran to the front where the petrol tanks were full and started furiously to shovel earth on to where the petrol was dripping down in the hope that it would restrict the spread of the flames. I still hope that what we did was of some use.

Eventually a shout advised us that Bill had been released from the turret. By this time an ambulance was in the lane. Both Bill Godfrey and Don Jennings were taken to hospital. When the rest of us left, the flames were fast spreading down the fuselage towards the rear and across the wings, all of which of course were covered in inflammable doped fabric.

Fradley camp looked the same on return. Why should I think that it would have changed? I had no idea at all. But I am sure that we, the survivors, had.

After sharing living quarters with Don for some time, occupying them on my own seemed rather unacceptable that evening. Later, Colin Beattie tapped on my door. Bill Godfrey had died. There was just four of us left of the crew. One decision I came to was that in my pre-flight preparations I would check that the astrodome would release easily every time I flew in the future. It was a commitment that I kept.

The day of young Bill Godfrey's funeral came and aircrew of many nations, particularly Australians, joined the remnants of the crew for the service at St Stephen's church in Fradley village. He is buried in the war graves section of the surrounding churchyard. Strangely enough only a few yards away is the grave of Joachim Schwarz, a Luftwaffe pilot who was shot down the previous year; all the rest are Allied airmen. My wife Daphne and I visited the cemetery over many years.

A new crew would now have to be put together. The question was, who with? It was not resolved immediately. The four of us were sent on seven days' leave. Departing Fradley camp with a freshly issued leave pass in a safe place in my pocket I headed towards the hospital where Don was nursing a broken ankle. He must have been unaware of his injury when he walked out of the front of the crashed aircraft and then collapsed to the ground some yards away, where I found him. I have tried to remember the name of this particular hospital, and Burtonwood comes to mind. Anyhow, he was recovering and pleased to have a change of company. I then had to make my way to Birmingham to take the London train. It was on this second stage of the journey that I had a very embarrassing moment. The bus conductor was coming round collecting fares when I found that I did not have sufficient coins in my pocket to pay for the fare, so I had to offer a one-pound note saying, 'I am sorry but I have only this.' His reply was to the effect that he would take the rest of the fares and come back. When he did so it was to say, 'That's all right, this lady has paid for your ticket.' She must have overheard my remark and thought I was stony-broke. What could I do but thank her very much for her kindness, when in fact I was sitting there most likely with more money in my pocket than she had in her purse.

The accident with the Wellington was not mentioned back at home, and on returning from leave I had hoped that the future of the depleted crew would have been decided during the preceding week, but this was not so. However, flying for me started again almost immediately, although with new pilots again drawn from those that I already knew, having been part of the same course since arriving at Lichfield. Pilot Officer Keith Douglas and Sergeant Jack Murray were the first pair – Jack soon became the constant name, to be accompanied, for varying periods, by Pilot Officer Mal Blunt and once more by Ralph Longmuir. Three staff pilots took an active part in our preparation for posting to a squadron and flew with us from time to time; they were the flight commander Squadron Leader Bamford, Flight Lieutenant Walker and Sergeant Peatfield.

All went well until 2 April, a morning take-off in Wellington 8949. I had been the navigator in the crew used to ferry it to Lichfield from its former base just over a week previously. Ralph Longmuir was at the controls this day, and as we climbed up away from the runway the pilots noted that the undercarriage had not locked in the up position. Was this just an electrical fault? We levelled off to make a circuit of the airfield and to test the mechanism by lowering the undercarriage for landing. It went down so far and then stopped. We now had the situation that it would not lock up or down. A repeat performance did not produce any improvement in the situation. Best let them know on the ground.

'Try climbing to a reasonable height, dive at a moderate angle and pull up the nose to see if the change in direction will swing the undercarrige into the locked position', was the advice given. Well of course it didn't. The flight commander came up in another Wimpy and flew very close underneath to have a look, but nothing was going to improve the situation. So we had to fly around to reduce the petrol load. In more than three hours the familiar landmarks became even more familiar. Then it was time to go down.

'Get into your crash positions. … Land on the grass at the side of the runway.' The approach was long, shallow and low. We crunched down on the field; the heavy bomb bay took much of the strain, the undercarriage and wheels just buckled under, the propeller blades bent as they dug into the ground and the two engines stopped dead. The crew climbed out of their various exits. Again, I used the astrodome, already open this time. The fire engine and ambulance crews were standing by, but fortunately they were not required. This time we all survived with no serious injury, just the odd bruise between us. And there was the handsome Wellington with its tall tail high in the air, slumped down on its belly going nowhere. There was going to be a right rumpus about this episode. I could see that coming, and I was right.

The outcome of the investigation was that the pilot had lifted the aircraft off the runway, signalled the undercarriage into the 'up' position, causing it to unlock, and then allowed the plane to bump once more on take-off before climbing away and gaining height in the normal way. Sitting at the navigator's table I am not sure that I was even aware of the double bump. However light the impact, then, it was sufficient to wreck the unlocked undercarriage.

We flew on the next day and again on the one after. Then the crew reduced down to five and we did not fly with Ralph Longmuir again. Australian Jack Murray was now approved as captain of the crew, which was now composed of his fellow countryman, rear gunner Jimmy Crocket, front gunner South African Ralph Webb and Ted Willey and myself, both RAF and wireless operator and navigator/observer respectively. Night flying across country took precedence over daytime practice and occasionally we took one of the screened pilots with us. All being sergeants enabled us to have an easy relationship in off-duty hours.

On 27 April we joined several other crews in the late afternoon for briefing for that night's flight. This was to be our first venture into the skies above occupied territory. The navigators plotted charts and maps for the specified route and worked out flight plans, while the other members of the crews carried out their own preparations. Just after 21.30 hours Jack Murray took us up into the night sky and set course for Belgium, climbing as we did so. Good visual positions were confirmed on crossing the coast at Aldeburgh and on the coast of Belgium, giving us an accurate run to the position upwind of Lille where we were to drop the leaflets generally known as 'Nickels'. Ted Willey and I were delegated to heave them out down the flare shoot. There was an enormous pile of them done up in bundles lying mostly on the bed. Even at 15,000ft it proved to be very warm work; perhaps some ten to fifteen minutes later the last bundle disappeared out of sight and we could set course for Charleroi, leaving Lille well supplied with useful-sized paper. There had been a little flak from the Lille area to let us know that we were observed, but that was all.

The journey across France continued to Amiens and then out to the mouth of the Somme and across the Channel to Shoreham, the Identification, Friend or Foe (IFF) system on, and across home territory back to Fradley, to land after a flight of six and a quarter hours. Each of the Wellingtons had been loaded with two 250lb bombs to drop during the flight, but there had been severe conditions placed on the use of them. We had passed over two aerodromes that were in use for we could see lights of aircraft on the move, even from our height. It was tempting to stir things up below, but as instructions had been specific regarding their use we brought the bombs back. Not at all willingly I might say.

On the whole it was a very gentle introduction to the active war zone. As we were probably the first aircraft to take off, perhaps the opposition had considered that we were a single intruder and not worth worrying about. In any event the OTU staff were pleased to see us back.

But what seemed to be a very satisfactory conclusion to the exercise, wasn't, as next morning we learned that ours was the only one of that group of aircraft to return to Lichfield that night. Two failed to reappear at all and were brought down presumably through enemy action and the remaining two or three all landed at bases elsewhere in this country. One of the two planes lost was that captained by Sergeant D.A. Dale, who had

Sergeant Jimmy Jewell, one of the navigators of our own course, on board. As a result of this first sortie, a crew due to leave in a few days were now short of a wireless operator and we had to surrender one of our own at a moment's notice. Ted Willey and I had formed a good working partnership during the past few weeks and we all had confidence in him. The original crew had virtually disappeared by now. We wondered who we would get to fill the vacancy. It was Sergeant R. Brooker who found himself transferred to Murray's crew and we were due to be posted away in a short while. The course at Lichfield wound up with a concentration of visits to the bombing range at Cannock Chase to polish up the skills acquired at Fingal in Canada.

So it was packing up time once again and each crew seemed to be going to a different destination. My own team had travel warrants made out to a station named as Barnetby in north Lincolnshire. It was likely that each crew was being posted to replace the immediate losses on the various operational squadrons.

Over the months that we had been at Lichfield many air force men and women had made friends there with the local residents. Don and I had encountered two or three such people and also been welcomed by the family at the Tudor restaurant. After Don went into hospital it was easier for Doreen and I to have a few dates and outings together, but the posting to Lincolnshire was going to change all that.

The day of departure came. Early in the afternoon, at Trent Valley railway station, the posted crews with their luggage were there, waiting; the train had yet to come. For some, several local friends had turned up, Doreen among them to say goodbye. The train arrived, kit and luggage were loaded. A brief goodbye and we were gone. Many would never see Lichfield again. One of our crew stayed there for ever.

Wellington Ic just after take off from RAF Lichfield.

Chapter 4

You Are Now Among Men My Son

For the last hour we had passed through places with such exotic names as Gainsborough, Kirton Lindsey, Brigg and now – 'Barnetby … Barnetby … Barnetby!' The railway porter's calls echoed along the platform and roused us into action. Soon all of the crew and their baggage were off the train to see that another similar group had emerged from the next carriage. One or two individual airmen also appeared and then disappeared into the station building and were away. They were obviously returning from leave and knew their way around. There was no transport laid on for the newcomers and we were certainly not going to walk with all the gear that we had with us. In any case, where was the aerodrome? None of us had been here before. The railway was on an embankment on one side of a wide valley; I imagined the station platforms situated above the valley floor could be bleak and cold with the winter winds whistling across the fields and villages. Although nowhere, I have concluded, could be as raw and desolate as the station perched above the Fens at Ely in midwinter, but at least at that location there was a warm and welcoming buffet open in which to wait for the connecting train. There was no such buffet here at Barnetby, but we did notice the pub on the opposite side of the station yard. Closed of course. Neither was there any sign of an RAF presence at all. For a brief period we had heard an aero-engine warming up in the distance, but it was difficult to make out from which direction it had come.

However, transport eventually turned up, so we were on our way again – down to the road where it ran under the railway, left up the hill past a WAAF camp and on to the top, and in a minute or two past the guard-room at the main entrance to the airfield. The access road stretched ahead

along the edge of a wood and across the approach to one of the runways; everything looked to be larger than I had ever previously seen
and this was only part of the whole. Round a corner and the rest of the
base came into view; it was indeed extensive, with Wellington aircraft
dispersed at intervals – the far boundary looked almost as if it could be
in the next county.

Jack Murray's crew were accommodated in a large Nissen hut not far
from the sergeants' mess; it was already partly occupied by another crew.
On the whole it looked reasonably comfortable, with a large round
upright iron stove in the middle of the floor. I wondered how many other
crews had lived there before us. Nobody ever said.

Our arrival date was 20 May 1941 and, little by little, we garnered information on our new posting. This was RAF Elsham Wolds in north
Lincolnshire, home to 103 Squadron, Bomber Command. The reason we
were here, though, was yet to be fully explained.

Next morning after breakfast in the mess we were off down to the
squadron HQ, following the general stream of NCOs. This was a long
wood hut beyond the line of hangars not far from the perimeter track.
Barely inside the building I ran into two other members from the same
course at Lichfield OTU – Sergeant W.J. Moss, a fellow navigator, and
Sergeant Ted Willey, who for quite a long time had been our wireless
operator. They had probably only been here for a couple of weeks or so
but what a difference that short time had made, for they were experienced,
assured and were obviously well established here in Sergeant S.J. Vickery's
crew. We had already met him on arrival last evening.

It was necessary to make ourselves known, eventually reaching the
squadron adjutant in his office. Then with formalities completed came
the interview with the squadron commander. I wondered what such a
man would be like. This was going to be an official approach in any
case. We drew to attention and saluted – good heavens it wasn't a stranger
after all, but Wing Commander du Boulay in the flesh. Until recently he
was chief instructor at 27 OTU, Lichfield. So he was virtually new here
too. I would have thought that the adjutant would already have briefed
him on where we came from, but not so. He asked the question and raised
a little smile on hearing that it was Lichfield, saying: 'You have been well
trained then?' We nodded perfunctorily. 'Sir.' 'Report to "B" flight com-

mander,' He instructed. 'That is all.' And that was it; another salute and we were dismissed.

In the few minutes we had been in with the adjutant and the CO the crew room had filled up with the aircrews and was alive with a buzz of confidence and expectancy. I felt that there was a long time to go and experience to be gained before becoming an equal part of this gathering. They were veterans and, above all, airmen.

However, there were things yet to do. In the first place we had to report to the 'B' flight office as ordered. Several pilots were coming out, but one remained there. We were introduced to Sergeant Staniland, who had been on the squadron for some time; he was experienced and from now on would be the senior pilot of our aircrew. Jack Murray was required to become familiar with the trials of operations, as indeed we all were, before becoming the captain of the crew. With the pilot's introduction concluded, the rest of us had to sort out our particular relationships in the parts we had to play. In my case it was with the squadron navigation leader and then on to the station navigation officer, at the same time gathering up the instruments, maps, charts and necessities to carry out my flying duties. This was all done and we were ready to enter the conflict. In the days following we flew with Sergeant Staniland as captain and Jack Murray in a new aircraft with the identification letters 'PM-L'; the L was always referred to as 'L for London', the PM, of course, being the squadron's own recognition letters. The aircraft was still a Wellington 1c, the backbone of Bomber Command up to that time, and much favoured by myself not only for its rugged strength but for the elegance of design, and it felt a comfortable space to work in.

In the last days of May a change was felt in the air. Additional planes and aircrews began to arrive from 22 OTU at Wellesbourne Mountford, adding to the congestion both in the domestic camp as well as that in the working areas. The engineering ground staff were being pushed to get all planes up to full flying condition. It looked as if a maximum operational effort was in the wind, but nobody was saying what.

On the morning of 30 May the hustle increased as air tests were carried out. Radio checks in all aircraft were made during the usual morning period. This was confined to set times throughout Bomber Command so that bursts of radio activity should not indicate to enemy listening stations that preparations for a raid were in hand. Petrol bowsers circled the airfield, refuelling the Wellingtons, while air gunners and armourers inspected gun turrets and bombloads were lifted into bomb bays. By this time the crew lists had been posted, so that we already knew that we were on for this operation. Navigators were warned of the time of their particular briefing in the afternoon.

Time fled by. This was an important step in the preparation programme; charts and maps had to be marked up and flight plans prepared. To do this full information had to be made known; consequently the navigators were among the first to be made aware of the target for that night. We were tense and ready in the nav. briefing room, where it was crowded and tables were drowning in a sea of charts and maps. At the far end of the room the wall was covered by a map of the whole of the European theatre of war, the detail obscured from view by a large blue curtain. The buzz of conversation and speculation ceased as the station nav. officer entered the room and made sure doors and windows were closed. This was the critical moment. As he swept the blue curtain aside, all was revealed. Eyes flashed to the end of the marker tape and the spot in Germany at its end. 'Cologne.' A collective 'Ah!' breathed its way over the chart tables, followed by 'Not bad then, not bad at all.' The way back was different to that to be followed on the way to the target, to avoid meeting head-on the aircraft still advancing, possibly to stretch the defences and perhaps a quicker way back to base.

Talk reduced to a murmur as each navigator got down to preparing his flight plan after laying out the direction to be followed on his Mercator's chart. With this route, the wind information from the Met. Office and the speed of the aircraft, he could calculate courses and times for each leg of the flight from take-off to landing back at Elsham. There were consultations between neighbouring navigators to ensure similarity of results and that no major errors occurred. Once in the aircraft you were on your own and fully occupied. Having to compensate for calculation errors increased the risk not only for oneself but the whole crew as well. There was also the situation that if the navigator was disabled there was ready for use sufficient information in the flight plan to get the aircraft back home, where there were facilities to assist.

'All done? Keep what you know to yourself.' The time of supper and main briefing was repeated and some thirty navigators now had to lock their bags of equipment and information away in their lockers and await the next stage. Sooner or later your pilot sought you out to discover where the crew were going that night if he hadn't already found out elsewhere. Well you worked together didn't you? He had his own opinions and thoughts on the target, which could colour his actions later when time was at a premium.

After a meal the time for the main briefing approached rapidly and the hall set aside for this purpose was overfilled with the crews of the many aircraft now awaiting the time of take-off. With the name of the station commander on the ops list something special was about to happen. Chair legs scraped on the wood floor as everybody stood up when Group Captain Constantine entered, followed by the various specialist officers who were to conduct the briefing. Those of us who had a seat sat down and the rest, well hard luck. This was the moment of truth when speculation came to an end. 'We are tonight taking part in an operation that for the first time puts more than one thousand aircraft over the target.' The group captain's words produced a roar of approval from the assembled aircrews, which took some moments to subside. The rest of the briefing followed the traditional form, with relevant information and facts for pilots by the squadron CO and by the radio, gunnery, navigation and engineering leaders as well as intelligence gen for all. Then spoke the duty Met. officer, whose promise of favourable weather conditions throughout was greeted by ironic cheers. He left the room smiling.

As the hall emptied each flyer was issued with a flat metal tin of emergency rations and money of the countries over which the operational aircraft would pass. The crowd of airmen surged along the camp roads to the squadron HQ to open up their lockers, dress, collect issued equipment and prepare for the flight. Transport to the aircraft at the dispersal points was ready and waiting outside. Now it was too late to have second thoughts. Now it was time to go.

'Who is next?' a WAAF driver called from the cab of her vehicle. 'Are we all here?' said Staniland, with the affirmative 'Yes' from the rest of us. 'L for London please' he indicated to the WAAF, and having scrambled aboard we sped off round the perimeter track to be dropped off at our dispersal point. How many times had she done this before? The Wimpy sat there like a terrier ready for the signal to be off. Not yet. First it was necessary to get the gear on board and for me to set out charts and instruments. Is the astrodome OK? Is the bombsight still in position? Is the bombload as we expect and is it on safe?! Then when each of us had done his bit it was a question of waiting for start-up time. Some flyers had rituals that they followed before every operation or even each flight; it must have been a routine that had a settling effect on the individual.

The countryside seemed to be holding its breath. It was dark now, and quiet – not even the whistle of a steam engine down at the station in the village. Those airmen who smoked took the opportunity in the last minutes of waiting. The ground crew who had put in long hours ensuring that the aircraft were in top condition hovered around a few yards away. Conversation was not wanted now. Then across the airfield the stutter of a Pegasus aero-engine turning over to start up caught the moment; as the seconds ticked by others joined in. We climbed the ladder into the nose of the aircraft, the flight mechanics called out 'Good Luck' just the once. Soon the skipper had the two engines throbbing as he went through the practice of checking that they were to his satisfaction; he then signed for the aircraft and the airman disappeared through the hatch. Brakes now off, the engines revved up enough to move us forward at little more than walking pace along the perimeter track towards the entry at the end of the runway in use. We were next; with thirty aircraft to take off there was no hanging about. Now it was our turn – the skipper swung the Wimpy on to the runway and lined it up down the long, wide strip of concrete. Brakes back on, the power is increased until the plane is straining against the brakes. Then it was brakes off again and we were on our way. The Wimpy surged forward. In seconds the rumble of the wheels eased, the undercarriage was raised and we were airborne. The end of the runway flashed past below, followed by the hedgerow on the side of the lane and then the edge of the wolds. The ground fell away and suddenly there was an extra 300ft of altitude above the level fields below. Height was gained as we turned back towards the airfield. Time of take-off was recorded in my log.

The skipper already had the first course to fly and called me when we passed over the centre of Elsham Wolds airbase. I noted the time of departure in the log and on the chart. What a tremendous night to make one's first operational flight with the squadron. Maplethorpe was far below. Soon IFF was switched off. At 10,000ft it was face masks on and we all switched on oxygen. More height was gained slowly until 15,000ft was indicated on the altimeter and we levelled off. I looked out for the point at which we crossed over the Belgian coast, logged the time and plotted it. Were we on course? The wind changed direction – a new course was needed, so it was calculated and given to the pilot to alter to in two minutes' time. We were now over occupied territory, and needed to keep a sharp lookout for fighters.

Departing from smooth, level flight, the skipper indulged in a move-ment resembling a corkscrew, changing the level of the aircraft and also its horizontal position from side to side in an endeavour to distract an enemy nightfighter pilot's aim if one was trying to sneak up on our tail. It was very disconcerting trying to plot courses on the chart while this was going on. And this continued all the way to the target. How did the rear gunner feel about being twirled around in the sky? In his turret he was not saying. I popped up into the astrodome to look around; there was nobody there – if we are one of a thousand where the devil were all the other aircraft?

The front gunner called up to tell us he had seen the reflection of moonlight on the river we have to cross; there was a large bend just to the south, so we got a good pinpoint to confirm our position and also to check our timing towards the target. In a few minutes I had a small change of course calculated and also an adjustment to our air speed to ensure that we arrived over Cologne on time. Another look around and there was a faint glow on the horizon ahead, little else other than some isolated flak up to our level. Ah! Over to the south a couple of miles away there was a bright ball of red, which exploded with a flash. It must have been one of ours. There were nightfighters about then, unless it was one of the German pyrotechnics. I took the time to enter the event in my log. More information came in for me; the wireless operator had got some loop bearings for me so I was busy for a time.

A check of the time on my watch and I called the pilot to inform him of how many minutes we had to go. His reply was to summon me up to the front to take a look. The light in the pilot's position was bright yellow and a mile or two ahead was Cologne, a sea of bright flares, trails of incendiaries, fires, flashes of high explosives and brief, intense bursts of brilliant light from the photographic flashes dropped for the camera in each attacking aircraft. Vast wands of searchlights swayed across the sky, sometimes locking on to a bomber at or above our level, to be followed by six or more joining to form a cone of light, with clusters of prickly stars of heavy flak trying to shoot it down. On occasions they succeeded, with an aircraft falling out of the sky in a tumbling jumble of burning metal, fabric and fuel, and men. It was a sobering sight.

I was now down in the nose of the Wimpy, bombsight set up, the bomb switches at the ready, looking forward for our aiming point. Trailing aerial was wound in and the bomb doors opened. I compared the scene before me against the target map in my hand. There was the square with the cathedral ahead. We were now flying straight and level. This was the time that our position in the sky could be predicted accurately by the anti-aircraft batteries below; were they on to us? In a few seconds we would know. 'Left … left skipper … steady … steady … right … steady.' Then with a press of the button, 'Bombs gone.' Relieved of its load the aircraft lifted in the sky. 'Flash gone', now it was straight and level. The photo was taken. The pilot changed direction, putting the nose of the aircraft down to increase speed, closed the bomb doors, and we hastened out of the target area and turned on to the first course for home. Very little flak now, but everyone looks out for fighters. 'Did anyone see that four-engined Halifax above us on the way in?' The response was 'No.' 'He was just over to starboard when he dropped his load.' We all agreed that was too close for comfort.

We seemed to be alone in the sky again. All the conflagration that was Cologne was beginning to recede into the distance. Height was gradually lost on this leg of the return and oxygen turned off. There was a blaze down on the ground – perhaps an aircraft fire – but no telling which side it belonged to; it may not have been one of ours. All the same I noted it down with the time. We swept onwards towards the Belgian coast; a little light flak shot up into the sky, looking like a string of red sausages. The problem there was that you could see the tracer ammunition but not the other three sorts in between. Clear again, our Wimpy headed out over the sea.

'Pilot here, where are we now navigator?'

'About halfway across skipper.'

'OK I'm altering course to 340° magnetic now.' Well, what could you do in respect of this instruction; after all he was captain of the aircraft and had experienced a considerable number of operations. He must have had good reason for this setting.

My reply was 'OK skipper.' It was no great problem for me; I converted the magnet course to a true bearing and amended the plotting chart, keeping a check on where we were heading. IFF was on. Still over the sea we flew up the east coast in a northerly direction as the sky lightened, eventually sweeping across the sandy beach of the Lincolnshire coast at a few hundred feet in the early morning light towards Elsham, probably waking a few local residents. We revelled in the open countryside just below and the peace that it represented to us, far from the tragedy that was Cologne.

The Nazis had been aggressive for years now and building up their navy, army and air force; it was time somebody stood up against them. Our lot weren't ready for a major fight were they? But now look at the result of our inactivity – the German army controlled the whole of the coastline of mainland Europe from the North Cape right down to the western end of the Pyrenees and Spain. What a mess we were all in; when would it all end?

It was time to pick up a few local landmarks. Just then a radio message was passed to me that we were to be diverted to the nearby aerodrome of RAF Kirmington. A small alteration of course by the pilot and 'L for London' was soon joining others in the landing circuit. Elsham was probably over-loaded with returning planes running low in fuel. Our turn now, we felt the undercarriage go down and also the flaps affecting the attitude of the plane on the approach; the wheels kissed the concrete, landed fully, and I logged the time. Suddenly the tiredness hit us – nearly a twenty-four hour day and we still have to fly back to Elsham.

Later that morning we landed safely back on Elsham's main runway, taxiing round the perimeter track and swinging round on to the hard-standing at our dispersal point. Engines off. It feels great to be home. Not so great for Sergeant Flowers and his crew, though, for they crashed on take-off at Kirmington with failure of the port engine. It was hard to imagine that they had successfully completed another major op, arrived safely back, only to be killed on a local transfer flight. Just two of the crew survived.

With our feet back on the ground, we gathered up charts, log and instruments into the navigation bag and placed the sextant in its box. Then with parachute, helmet and whatever else came to hand it was out through the trap door in the nose of the aircraft and backwards down the ladder. The camp was like a small town and each crew was part of a community, so every time you left you came back 'home'. At least you believed you would. Some didn't.

Soon transport swept up to the hardstanding; it was the same WAAF who brought us out the night before. With a smile she said: 'You're back then, ready to go?' We were. Having put our gear away in the lockers it was off to the debriefing room. There was a queue of crews awaiting their turn to be interviewed, with mugs of tea to hand. The pilot of each team gave a general run through of the events experienced and then each crewmember added his own details. My log and navigation chart were retained by the navigation officer, particular interest being directed to the additional notes and times made of incidents observed during the course of the flight.

By now there was little attempt to hide the sense of weariness and tension, and whatever the time on the clock, it was breakfast time. There was barely an urge to do more than take a leisurely meal, until the desire for bed became more urgent and the mess emptied in response. And that was that until the next time. I hoped we would not be on again that night, but somebody would be.

The 'Thousand Bomber' force stayed together and on the third night we flew to Essen. To me events seemed to be following a similar pattern to those of the Cologne trip. While the large bomber force dispersed, with those from the OTUs returning to their bases, the operational squadrons continued the pressure on German targets with several raids on Essen, Bremen and Emden in quick succession. The 'Thousand Bomber' force was reassembled for another raid on Bremen later in the month. Cloudy conditions were forecast and we found almost complete cover in the target area. A few gaps were seen and we did manage to bomb through one from 8,000ft; down at this level the flak was heavy and troublesome. I thought later that because of the adverse weather conditions we were less successful than previously.

By this time I was with Flying Officer Frith and his crew. Earlier in the month Jack Murray had been posted to 460 Squadron, it being an Australian unit. I suspect that he had asked for the move to join his countrymen. In addition, our own skipper, Sergeant Staniland, had been promoted to commissioned officer rank and promptly disappeared elsewhere. So our crew disbanded and – as I had – those left joined other crews who were short of a member.

Following a night operation there was always the possibility of being sent off in daylight to search an area in the North Sea for dinghies with men in them from aircraft downed in the sea. Sometimes, instead of working as part of a flight of four or five aircraft flying in line abreast, we would scan the designated area several times in isolation. At times of poor visibility many changes of course were required to adequately observe the area and were spread over several hours. During this period a variation in the wind could lead to some loss of accuracy in our position and radio bearings became of great use. Fortunately, on one such occasion, I had just plotted some radio bearings that indicated that we were close to the Dutch coast; it was a warning to be particularly alert. The bearings were good, for when we nosed out of the bank of low cloud into sunshine there on the horizon was the near coast of Holland. For a period we had been blown in an easterly direction. We completed the search and set course back towards our own base. Perhaps we had been lucky not to have been intercepted by the Luftwaffe, but it did show the desperate need for accurate position-finding equipment for use in adverse conditions.

For the last few weeks the navigators had been spending non-flying hours in a wooden building, which was staffed by several Canadian technicians and locked to everybody else. Inside the building the equipment was one of the new navigation aids known as 'Gee'. Within the limitations of being stationary it was necessary for us to become proficient in its use. The airborne equipment was not fitted into the Wellingtons with which we were operating, but simulated exercises under the control of the technicians prepared the navigators for the time when this would be so. Perhaps this was the answer to position finding at night or in conditions of poor visibility, or out over the sea for hours.

It was known that a change in the aircraft supplied to the squadron was to be implemented. The Wellington 1c types were an early design and since their introduction there had been design advances giving improved performance. With the beginning of July the new planes began to arrive and take the place of the twin-engined Wellington. We could now see the successor – a black monster with four engines, a gaping bomb bay and a multiple tailplane. It was a Handley Page Mk. II Halifax.

A Heavy Conversion Unit (HCU) was formed from one of the flights at Elsham under the command of an officer who had already completed the conversion process. The squadron pilots started the course to convert on to the new aircraft. In the meantime, the remaining crewmembers were also required to bring themselves up to date; this involved being posted elsewhere for a week or so. My first flight in a Halifax was as the navigator with Squadron Leader Holford ferrying a number of bomb aimers up to RAF Lossiemouth for a course. This must have been the first Halifax to land there for it created considerable interest and required a guard until the time came to fly home, leaving the bombardiers to receive their training. The flights out and back gave me the opportunity to use the Gee equipment for the first time in the air and I was most impressed with its performance.

Shortly afterwards I was also flown to RAF Pocklington, base for 102 Squadron, for a brief period to expand my experience with the Gee equipment. After my return to my base at Elsham Wolds, and with no crew existing, I now flew with many of the squadron's pilots, both as a navigator and also in a teaching mode for this new navigation aid. My various pilots included Squadron Leader Fox, Flight Lieutenant Frith, Pilot Officers Gilby and Staniland and, among the senior NCOs, Flight Sergeant Arthur Tilley. The last named had been an acquaintance for some time before my coming to Elsham.

With the changeover of the aircraft my opportunities for the occasional dual instruction at the aircraft controls disappeared. But for some time I had been well acquainted with the flight sergeant who was in charge of tuition on the ground-based alternative, the Link Trainer. Under his voluntary tutelage of an evening, I managed to produce acceptable results.

This was indeed only an insurance should we be faced with our pilot being put out of action at any time after we resumed operations.

During the month of July many new aircrew joined the squadron. With the new aircraft, extra crew were needed to operate the Halifax, at least seven being required in total. The additions were a flight engineer plus a mid-upper gunner for greater defensive power. It was therefore during the first days of August that the composition of the new crew make-up was revealed. The information that the new crew lists had been posted up spread rapidly and those not already down at the squadron headquarters made their way there as soon as possible. The first action was to scan each list to pick out your own name, next to identify your new pilot and then the rest of the crew. Our team comprised Warrant Officer Edwards, Flight Sergeant Hawthorn, Flight Sergeant MacDonald, Flight Sergeant Stolz-Page, Sergeant Green, Sergeant Richards and me. I had a strong idea who our pilot Warrant Officer Edwards was, but not the others. Right, it was best to find our new pilot and captain first of all. This done, the other names of the crew began to gain faces and soon the introductions were completed. How lucky could you get? Four of those named were of the regular air force; other details came out as the days went by. The Halifax aircraft that had been allocated to us was 'PM-Q' generally known as 'Q for Queenie' and number W1216.

Now we had to find out if we could work together. This was imminent, for our first flight together was a sea sweep at a fairly low level lasting six and a half hours. Well that, as a test of personalities, was looked upon as a success as well as building up our confidence in the aircraft.

Then everybody's confidence took a hard knock.

Many crews were flying and the squadron block was quiet. I was in the office talking to two of the pilots when a great roar of four Merlin engines on full power drowned the background murmur of aircraft cruising in the vicinity of the airfield. Looking out of the windows we had the horrific sight of a Halifax, nose down, with the fuselage and wings vertical and heading straight for the ground. One of my companions shouted, 'That plane is going to crash!' We immediately rushed outside into the full blast of the engine noise. It was only a few hundred yards away; the pilot was obviously using full power to try and bring the nose up, but to no avail. The aircraft disappeared behind the trees and hedge at the boundary of the airfield and the impact occurred at the edge of the wolds, into farmland at a lower level. There was sudden and complete silence as we lost view and stood there unable to move. Many seconds passed and then came a vast pillar of ugly black smoke rapidly rising high to stain the sky. There had been members of an additional crew on board as well. Twelve young aircrew died that day.

Flight Sergeant Gordon Mellor, September 1942

Chapter 5

Feet Back on the Ground

During the first two weeks of August 1942 the squadron completed the conversion period and rejoined the front line of Bomber Command. On the 16th of that month Warrant Officer Edwards and his crew took to the air on their first operation together. This was to Düsseldorf with a full load of incendiaries. Arriving in the Ruhr we found there was a wide scattering of cloud, more than expected; however, we picked a break between the clouds and saw the target below. The escape from the target area and the return to base did not produce anything unusual, other than we appeared to be low on fuel. To ensure that we had sufficient the skipper decided to land once we were back in home skies and take on a supplementary amount. I gave him the new course and we landed at RAF Docking at about 5.30 in the morning. This took some little time to arrange so Elsham was notified that we would be along later. The squadron CO was not pleased about this and said so.

By now, of course, we had got used to the higher airspeed of the Halifax, which reduced the time available for navigation between turning points. It was the application of the Gee (TR1335) system that had a beneficial effect on my input on the Düsseldorf operation for a significant part of the route to the target. The German opposition was finding ways of jamming the system to the extent that the interference over Holland made it increasingly impossible to get the three readings required; on the return journey we gradually flew out of the area and the signals consequently improved with every mile between us and mainland Europe. In addition, I was beginning to develop a system for checking the forecast winds that we had been given during briefing by the meteorologists while the flight progressed from low level in the early stages up to the operating level at 15,000ft or more. On one or two occasions I was asked to fly with newly arrived navigators to provide assistance in operating the Gee system until they had grasped its practical possibilities.

Operations continued to be flown to various targets such as Kassel, Nuremberg, Düsseldorf and Bremen, with some return visits. Daytime flying continued. Some were still training flights for simulated air-to-air gunnery; others were for bombing practice. The squadron CO changed – Wing Commander du Boulay left and Wing Commander Carter took over as his replacement. He promptly joined us for an evening flight, taking off in daylight and then returning for a flarepath landing after dark.

There were also changes to our crew despite its recent formation. Our Canadian wireless operator, Flight Sergeant Don Macdonald – who completed his tour and had been awarded a DFM for events with another crew while on Wellington aircraft – was posted away from Elsham, but we did keep in touch for very many years. This had been followed by rear gunner Flight Sergeant Stolz-Page being transferred to another crew. In a brief time we lost two very experienced airmen and were faced with two newly arrived replacements. The first was Sergeant Doug Giddens from New Zealand as radio operator, then Sergeant Norman McMaster, who took up the vacancy in the rear turret. They fit in with the rest of us very well and took their first operations after-wards; once again the seven of us were happy with the combination of nationalities.

As a crew we had an occasional visit down to the Railway Hotel in Barnetby for an entertaining evening, walking both ways, or to more distant Scunthorpe on the camp bus for a film or for shopping, finish-ing up at the Oswald for a quick drink and then a scramble to catch the last bus returning to camp. Most of us had a bicycle, or the use of one, which put Brigg and Barton-upon-Humber within reach. Grimsby was a train journey away and not a popular venue at all. I went once with one of the crew but it was not a great success.

September slipped into October, with a raid to Krefeld of less than 200 aircraft, which followed the general pattern. While strongly defended with heavy flak, it was remarkable for the searchlights, which were in a large and very bright concentration. This was followed three days later on 5 October with another modest raid of some 250-plus aircraft. On that day during the late morning and afternoon the occasional rumble of thunder was heard in the distance, but the navigator's briefing was called as usual and the target for that night revealed with the drawing back of the blue curtain. It proved to be Aachen and little more than 15 miles into Germany from Belgium. It was the route that was the surprise, for the red string marking the track to be followed from Elsham stretched southwards, just east of London, over Kent and across the Channel to a point in France, then a left-hand turn and directly on a long, straight leg to that German city. The early Met. forecast indicated that the winds might be tricky but flight plans were completed and that was it for the moment. Pilot Sergeant Mead was joining us for his first operational experience with the squadron.

The pre-flight hours passed as usual until it was time for the main briefing when all crews on ops attended for the vital presentation of all necessary information. The route was the same as that given to the navigators some hours previously and gave cause for whispered comment; however, item followed item with few remarks until the senior Met. officer concluded his contribution by saying that we could expect to run into one or two thunderstorms. As usual his statement raised a cheer and laughter. I often thought this was his attempt to reduce the tension built up during the briefing.

Outside the squadron HQ building, waiting for transport to take us out to the aircraft, the atmosphere felt heavy and out of humour, not only with the murmuring of distant thunder from a cold front but, to me among the assembled aircrews, perhaps it was just my imagination, unsettling all the same. But routine took over, and with the setting out of charts and equipment, checking the navigation aids and putting the parachute into its storage place, it filled in the time before start-up of engines. That first ghostly cough and splutter in the distance across the airfield from the engines of the first plane to be off sent a momentary twitch down the spine and pulled the attention to the job in hand. Soon our aircraft was rolling along the perimeter track of the airfield to the beginning of the long flarepath and that acceleration into the night sky.

Height gained, the aircraft turned and headed back over the runways on the first course; the east coast was unseen way over to port and, even though we had gained more height, that great indent of the Wash in the coastline was lost in the dark. London was quiet tonight, no searchlights or guns disturbed the sky. Eyes were now wide open for the English Channel. Thunderstorms had been a problem, giving us a bumpy ride and the occasional brilliant flash in the mid-distance. Despite the electrical interference I felt that the weather had eased somewhat as we travelled south, but the sky was completely overcast so that the darkness was almost impenetrable. However, the sea in the Channel did show up a lighter shade of grey than the land and my navigation calculations had a visual check. Over France, having turned towards Belgium and Germany beyond, the cloud cover lightened and we broke through the overcast into clear skies and starlight at our level. There was still an amount of cloud below but this was diminishing and once it dispersed altogether the Halifax would be less noticeable against a land background than when there was white cloud beneath. Opposing fighters were the initial concern and a sharp lookout was maintained.

The minutes passed, and to all appearances we were alone in the sky; there was only the occasional flash of flak some distance away to starboard on a parallel line to our track, so there must be fighters about. It was on this long leg that our pilot first made us aware of a change in the firmament above and that we were being treated to a glorious display of the Northern Lights. A gossamer veil of pulsating light covered a large part of the sky to the north of us, looking as if the display extended to infinity; perhaps it did. I had only once experienced anything approaching its equal before, while at Fingal in Canada, and even so I was not sure that it was such a magical moment as this.

The miles slipped away, with Eddie Edwards our pilot keeping the Halifax manoeuvring in a spiral like a corkscrew to reduce the risk of being surprised with a fighter attack. Fortunately we were left alone. 'How are we doing Nav?' came Eddie's voice over the intercom. I gave him the distance still to go to the target and the time it would take. He then asked me to come up and take a look, as my forward vision at the navigation table was rather limited. All appeared much as I would expect, except there was a wide glow extending along the horizon. It couldn't be the very early stages of sunrise as it was too early for dawn, so it must be the result of the bombers in front of us. Gradually, as we drew closer to the time over target and as the miles sped by, it became obvious that it was indeed the planned attack, but it didn't look as if it was going to plan. From close up we could see that it stretched some 20 miles wide. flares were going down all over the place; there were some target markers well spaced out. It was a shambles. The front gunner, 'Twiggy' Hawthorn, called out that we were not heading towards the target. I knew that we were a little north of our track. He and I had a quick chat and agreed with the skipper that we should turn towards the southern end of the area under attack. Soon positive signs came in view to confirm that it had been the right decision. There was little flak as we swept across Aachen, where some others had obviously recognised the correct target area and attacked.

At slightly less than 12,000ft we made our second approach to the aiming point. The trailing aerial was wound in, bomb doors were opened, and then our load was unleashed. This was the period of flying straight and level, and the most dangerous. The brilliant photo-flash went off well below and Eddie could now take evasive action, but we had already been spotted and two thumps of heavy flak nearby jolted the whole aircraft. With the nose of the Halifax down we raced out of the target area into the comparative darkness as fast as possible, thence to swing round on to our exit course and so head for home.

No more than two minutes later Norman McMaster's voice came over the intercom saying that there was an Me110 formating upon us about 500yd to the rear. The question was, should we open fire on him first in the hope that it would scare him off? In the meantime, I fired off the German triple-star colours of the day already loaded in the Very pistol in the roof of the Halifax. Would this deter the Luftwaffe pilot from attacking or at least leave him in some doubt so that we could slip away? No it would not, for he followed the twists and turns that Eddie put our aircraft through. With the aircraft in a suitable position with both the rear and mid-upper turrets bearing upon the Me110, the gunners opened fire. Did they hit it? We would never know. The German pilot was no beginner for he stayed out of effective range of the .303 Browning guns in the turrets and also sank lower so that the mid-upper gunner was unsighted and could not help to defend the rear of our plane. His further response was to fire cannon shells into the Halifax. The result for us was a disaster for both inboard engines were struck and set on fire.

Norman in the rear turret was hit, and a further two bursts of bright yellow balls of flame swept through either side of the fuselage, creating more damage and destruction to the body structure and the wings. How six of the crew in the nose of the bomber could escape with their lives was beyond belief at that moment. The aircraft was fast losing height, with fires fuelled from the wing tanks roaring in the slipstream. Getting back to England was not possible. Eddie ordered: 'Everybody out, abandon aircraft.' I handed Eddie's parachute up to Mark Mead the second pilot to help him clip it on while still controlling the plane. The entry hatch in the nose under our feet was lifted and dropped out. No hanging about now, Eddie could not leave his position until we had all gone.

With parachute clipped on it was my turn to go. I sat down on the edge of that gaping hole with my back to the nose of the aircraft and put my legs down into the slipstream of air rushing past beneath and stretched my hands towards the opposite edge of the opening to prevent my head hitting the other side. Before I could get them there I received an almighty shove on my back and I was out in the slipstream. With a momentary glimpse of the tailplane I fell and was jerked painfully into an upright position as the parachute opened, arresting my fall. I looked around trying to see the burning plane, but there was no sign of it. Where on earth had it gone? I deduced I must have been still facing the wrong way, with my back to it. Looking around it was starlight with a glimpse of moonlight and not an artificial light to be seen. Downwards there was a hazy blue vista of what looked like large balls and they were coming closer fast. I realised it was a mass of treetops and then I was crashing through the upper branches, to be brought to a sudden halt with my legs swinging free above the ground. The question now was, how far was I off the ground?

Nothing seemed real to me at all, and for a few seconds I couldn't grasp the fact that I must have made a safe landing; looking up I could see the white canopy of the parachute draped over the tree that I was hanging from. Without any visible evidence – for I couldn't even see my feet – I twisted the release lock on the parachute harness and pressed the button; the straps flew open and I dropped to the grass below. To my surprise I must have descended no more than 12in at the most. I still had the pull handle to activate the parachute in my hand, but there was no recollection of pulling it or counting to the recommended number first.

I was no longer attached to the parachute or the harness that had held me safely throughout the drop. My immediate action was supposed to be to gather up the parachute gear and bury it, or hide it at least. A few tentative tugs had no result and a more aggressive action did not improve the situation – the noise I made started dogs barking close by. I stopped pulling and kept still; the barking gradually subsided as they lost interest. In the meantime, I could see enough to come to the conclusion that as large as the trees were, the regular spacing indicated that I was in an old orchard and the dogs must be at a house nearby. It would be best for me to leave soon – I did not fancy fending off two guard dogs. So I climbed through a gap in the adjoining hedge. Beyond, the grassland sloped away gently towards the left. Instinctively I set off down the slope and after possibly 100yd slid down a bank on to a paved road, which also was on a slope. Of course I chose the down-hill route then wished I hadn't, for within a few seconds I was passing a house with a large hardstanding in front of it. This in itself was OK but there was a dark group of some six or seven people there looking up at the yellow glow in the sky; no doubt it was from the raid. Was I still in Germany? I couldn't turn back; all I could do was continue walking straight past them. Thankfully nobody challenged me and I disappeared into the night.

Walking along I now considered my options. I wasn't sure which country I was in – Holland, Belgium or Germany all had borders adjoining each other. We had changed direction so often in the encounter with the Me110 that it was impossible to know within 20 or so miles our exact position; added to that, how far had my parachute drifted? So I looked up at the sky to spot the North Star –there it was up front, so I was walking north. Was this the right thing to do? There was all of the North Sea and the English Channel between me and home. Denmark and Norway were both occupied, so no good walking in the direction of those countries. It had to be south or west; Spain seemed to be the best bet. I couldn't go back past that group of people. Ahead from where I was standing the road forked into two, both northerly routes. To the left was what looked like a cart track cutting through the bank to the higher ground, roughly to the west; that was the way to go. I stumbled along the uneven rising track and suddenly came to a halt – there were lights to my left among the twigs and rough undergrowth of the bank. Where on earth were they coming from? My imagination worked over-time; I even thought of light escaping from an underground building. As I got closer and closer I was startled to find the answer – the pinpricks of light were glow worms! This was my first, and only, time of seeing this phenomenon. Were they perhaps a omen that this was the right way to go? I walked on, the banks on either side diminishing in height until the cart track was level with the surrounding fields.

This was now wide-open farmland and my attention was immediately drawn to a bright orange fire in the distance, but how far away? It was difficult to judge. It was the only light to be seen and by contrast made the night seem darker. I was recovering my awareness and my hearing; the sound of ammunition exploding reached me and could only have come from the fire ahead of me, in all likelihood the remains of Halifax PM-Q burning away there. Could anything be done there? It must have been all of a mile or so away and probably crashed within minutes of our bailing out. Did we all get out?

Standing there, rooted to the spot, I could think of little else. Gradually my senses returned and I became aware of the vastness of the surrounding open countryside. The darkness of the land merged with sky with no visible horizon and as my gaze lifted to look into distant space the enormity of my situation hit me and I felt more alone than I had ever experienced before. A couple of minutes later the depression had passed, and I realised that this sequence of events had been at the back of my mind for months and now it had happened. I had already made my deci-sion, it was time to get on with it. There was nothing that anyone could do about the crash and the fire, so I turned away with the purpose of leaving the area as soon as possible. The German forces would already be looking for possible survivors. Commotion from the ammunition still exploding in the burning wreck, mingled with that of a vehicle some-where along a road near the crash site, nullified other sounds. I was making a little noise myself with my legs brushing rows of cabbages in the field. Suddenly, there was somebody else in the field close by. I stopped and knelt down so that I should not be seen; the other person finding that he was the only one moving also stopped. He remained unseen and after a while was heard to shuffle away. I stayed close to the ground until his sounds receded in the distance.

Now was the time to make my way out of the area, and keeping off the roads for the time being I headed in my chosen direction. As the night progressed it became necessary to use lanes that seemed convenient, having had trouble on several occasions with barbed-wire fencing. Even in the early morning hours the occasional cyclist suddenly approached, with a dim front lamp showing, leaving me scant time to hide in a nearby ditch. Fortunately they proved to be dry in most cases. I thought daylight was fast advancing and I now had to find a hiding place to use. Taking a footpath through some cultivated patches I found what I thought would serve my purpose. Two fields adjoined each other at different levels and were separated by a bank covered with a copse of trees and a thick undergrowth of bushes. I lodged myself out of sight in the latter and fell into a weary sleep.

Some time later I awoke stiff and cold to find there was a thick early morning mist, but as the sun broke through the general temperature rose and the mist cleared away. My spirits improved too, and out came the farmhands along the farm road through the field just below me and also in the field above me. I could hear them working and talking most of the day. It was with some relief that I was not discovered.

During the day I examined the contents of the escape tin that had been distributed to each member of the crew. Being only about the size of a fifty-cigarette tin the contents were surprisingly varied, from a rubber water container to Horlicks and water purifying tablets, a map and money of France, Belgium and Holland. I always carried a map of Europe in my pocket while flying over the occupied countries and studying this took up much of my time on this first day. Other than general farm noises only an occasional car on the road on the other side of the field in front of me disturbed the quiet, until a two-carriage tram unit rushed along the track running along the opposite edge of the road. It's two-toned horn announced its imminent arrival before disappearing in the direction of a town. I was not able to establish its destination.

Being October the hours of daylight were beginning to grow less and the temperature to drop. The farm workers were returning to the farm buildings, but I had to contain my impatience until most of the light had gone from the sky; even so, I was on my way before it was fully dark. Using the same tactics as the previous night, walking through the countryside on roads whenever possible, I even passed through villages undetected. Each morning it was necessary to find a hiding place. There were no set rules to follow; during the hours before dawn visibility was minimal, so keeping away from populated areas seemed obvious but not always possible. I came to the conclusion that finding a refuge was just luck. One particular early morning, having passed through a settlement and disturbed more than one dog with my footsteps, I found myself on a road running down quite a steep hill. Looking for a temporary shelter for the day I turned off into a narrow field. In the misty grey light I became aware of a long rickety fence with gardens running downhill on the far side. Thinking there might be a disused shed at the top of one of these gardens I looked around and found a small cave cut into the side of the hill, just big enough to lie down among some fruit boxes; it was obviously a store place.

I had been very lucky once again.

Later, after the mist had disappeared, I could see the houses at the bottom of the sloping gardens, a road and a small river along the valley floor, a railway and station on the far side and a road curving around the opposite hillside. All these landmarks agreed with the map that I had always carried with me in my pocket. I finally had an accurate idea of where I was. When night fell I walked downhill to the road at the bottom. Knowing there was a river there I crossed a narrow strip of grass with the intention of filling my water bottle. However, the riverbank was steep and some 5ft high; not only would I get my feet and trousers wet but getting up the bank would be most difficult. The idea had to be abandoned, so I returned to the road and made my way through the outskirts of the small town of Glons and up to the level crossing next to the railway station. There seemed to be no guard or railwayman on the crossing, so having watched other people pass over the tracks I followed suit and then on to the road curving round the hillside that I had seen from my view-point during the day. It was this very road that I had matched up with the map.

The road wound its way up the gradient and gradually evened out to a gentle undulation; good progress was made along this stretch, but having passed through the village of Paifve I found there was a tendency to bear east. I decided to turn off the road and cross the fields in the hope of finding another route more in keeping with my plans. This was partially achieved in that the new highway was more suitable for me in its direction. It appeared to be very straight and, I thought, heading directly for Liège so that I could turn off after a while and pass through the country just to the north of that city. I was depending on my memory for I could not consult the map in the darkness. Events followed as I hoped, for I was able to turn on to another good road into the small town of Lantin. Passing along one of the streets I noticed a house with a light showing through a gap in the curtains; I had a quick peer into the room, but nobody was to be seen. This had been easy to do for the front wall of the house and windows were right up to the back of the pavement, but it was not wise to stay there so I moved on round a corner to another street. Walking quietly along the pavement I suddenly heard water running; I had not had a drink for a whole day and it was urgent to do so. I decided to see if there was a reliable supply. The noise seemed to come from a passageway between two houses and, indeed, some yards up the alleyway water was running from a pipe into a water butt. It tasted all right and I intended to fill my water bottle from the storage barrel. I was leaning over the water butt, which was half in shadow from the next house and half in moonlight, when I heard the crunch of boots on the road and there right at the entrance to the alley, some 20ft away, stood a man in uniform looking my way with an occasional glance up and down the road. If I moved he would see the movement, even if now he only saw me as a part of the shadows. Surely he must know that I am here. I stood very still for what seemed like an hour. Eventually he went off up the road on his rounds. That was too close for comfort! I now needed that drink of water more than ever.

Further down the street I found a bombed house, again the front wall close on to the pavement; access was not difficult and I made my way up the staircase to the first floor, skirted round a large hole in the wood floor and settled down to sleep under the front windows. When I woke up it was daylight and the street below was busy with people and remained so all day. At one period two schoolboys came into the ground floor to play, but other than throwing bricks up through the hole in the ceiling on to the floor that I was standing on, did not come up the stairs. Obviously my situation was not as secure as I had hoped; indeed, if anyone had entered the building and climbed the stairs I would be discovered, for it was just a single room within four bare walls.

Soon after darkness fell the pedestrians made their way home and there were few people on the streets; now was the time to leave town. My route was along the main thoroughfare and I soon found myself leaving properties behind for more open country. It was very dark with an overcast sky; a few heavy spots of rain gave me warning that a wet night was possible. However, it was necessary to press on, hoping it would pay off; there was little other option left to me. Shortly afterwards, the break after the first few drops suddenly came to an end and the heavens opened with a deluge. Thick as the RAF uniform was it soon became very wet. Now a decision was called for – did I continue and trust that the rain would soon be over or did I return to the bombed house to dry off during the next day? I hated the idea of going back for I was going to lose a night's walking distance. Additionally, when daylight came all my hiding places would probably be soaking wet, which would not be good for a stay of many hours. So it was with a heavy heart that I turned and retraced my steps.

Passing back into the outskirts of Lantin the rain was certainly easing off when my attention was drawn to a faint gleam of light in an upstairs window of a house. I was coming to the conclusion that at my current rate of progress it would take months to get to Spain and then to Gibraltar. I had not eaten anything for days, other than indigestible raw potatoes from the fields and the Horlicks tablets from my escape tin. Should I knock on the door to see if I could dry off and hope that some food might be offered as well? Or would I be handed straight over to the authorities? After nights of walking and days of hiding, avoiding all contact with anybody, this would be a complete reversal of my approach to my predicament. I hovered in the darkest shadows with my thoughts racing, both with the desire for help but equally with the doubt of what the occupants of the house might do if they were unsympathetic or even hostile to my approach. At this very moment my whole future was in the balance.

Which course of action was it to be?

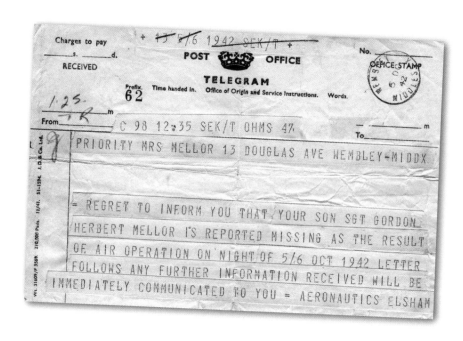

'Regret to inform you.'

Chapter 6

Family of Friends

Still with misgivings, and with much hesitation, I stood at the entrance. Finally I knocked on the front door. The window upstairs opened. A man's head popped out with the question 'Qui est la ?' – 'Who is there?' In a quiet voice I tried to explain that I was RAF and could do with some help. The window shut smartly and I sensed somebody coming downstairs. The front door was gingerly opened, with the question again as to who I was. It became obvious that I had to quickly allay his fears so I produced my badges of rank and brevet saying 'RAF' again and indicating the unfaded marks on my uniform where the badges had been removed. The effect was electric. The door was pushed open and I was hastily invited in. The light in the back room was switched on and I was confronted by the occupier, a small, grey man, possibly in his late forties. Within a minute he was joined by his wife, a lady of comfortable proportions. With a mixture of French, English and gestures all was made known. I was seated close to the large tiled stove in the corner of the room to dry my clothes and given hot food and ersatz coffee as the wet gently steamed out of my uniform.

I now found out who my benefactors were. The family name was Van Meeuwen and they had a young son, Jean, who was some ten years old. He attended the local school. This was a complication for he must not see me or be aware of my calling there; it would be quite easy for him to mention it inadvertently to his schoolfellows. If word got around the retribution would be swift and harsh. Sitting in the warmth beside the heating stove it was difficult not to fall asleep, for I was going to have to move on shortly; with luck the heavy rain would have stopped by then. I must have momentarily closed my eyes as I suddenly jerked wide awake to find that Monsieur Van Meeuwen had prepared to shave off my facial growth of several days. The warm water, the soap and brush, and the clean-shaven appearance was the ultimate luxury to be savoured for a few brief moments of sheer contentment.

I was unaware that they had already sent for help until there was a knock on the front door. They had made contact with their parish priest, Vicaire Adons, who entered the room and greeted me with a broad smile and a handshake and saying 'Goodbye' in English instead of 'Hello', before revealing that he was a fan of Arsenal Football Club. It was agreed that I should go with him and thus maintain the secrecy of my visit. The Van Meeuwens were true patriots and without question they had put the safety and the lives of the whole family in jeopardy for an unexpected and complete stranger who had merely identified himself with a couple of badges and the word 'RAF'. Even though our acquaintance was of only a few hours, it was a sad parting for obviously it would be a long time before we saw each other again.

As it was now later than the curfew hour, the Vicaire said that we would take the back paths to his home in the village of Alleur. For himself, he had a pass in order for him to visit his parishoners during the late hours. If we were challenged by the military he would still be compromised by my company. I was very concerned over this because during my talk with the Van Meeuwens they had disclosed that there was a German military encampment adjoining the road that I had walked along on my first venture from Lantin and returned past in the rainstorm. I had not seen it, nor had they seen me. Obviously there was a strong military presence in the neighbourhood. But with luck on our side, the Vicaire and I walked to Alleur without incident.

His house stood opposite the church, with its tall spire dominating the surrounding properties. We found his housekeeper still up, late as it was, and was introduced to her. When told that I was there to stay she took the news with calm and almost resignation. I was shown into a bedroom with a large bed covered with vast bedclothes and balloon pillows. The invitation was irresistible. This was my first night in a continental bed.

Vicaire Adons did not appear until mid-morning the next day, when he returned from his early duties to the church and community. He was obviously a busy man but managed to take on side issues as they occurred;

my being there was one such event. He told me that I would be enter-
tained during the afternoon by a lady who spoke English, as he was not
available. After lunch my visitor arrived, and indeed the two or so hours
that we spent together passed quickly; she was attractive, probably aged
about thirty-five, and did have very good command of the English
language. It was while we discussed venues in London that I came to the
conclusion that this was no innocent chat to while away an afternoon –
this was a searching enquiry to make sure that I was who and what I
said I was and not a plant to infiltrate forces opposed to the German
occupation. She also took my name, rank and number, next of kin and
home address, saying that sometimes a message could be passed on. I
do not remember her name – in fact I am not sure that she revealed it –
probably the best thing was to withhold it. We parted on the best of terms,
but there was no doubt in my mind that there was a local organisation
that had fingers spread out in all directions around Liège and by extraordinary luck when I knocked on the Van Meeuwen's door I had brushed
its fingertips.

Before long the Vicaire returned, animated and bright-eyed. Ah, I
thought, I had passed the test. His first remark confirmed this impression for he told me that I would be moving on that evening; I learned
later to Liège. To be sure, after dark there was another caller who you
would not look twice at in the street. I have found since then that I have
the same ability but, compared with this man, my height was a giveaway. However, he produced a long raincoat to put over my uniform; I
was already wearing a collar and tie so the result looked good – well good
enough to go out into dimly lit places. It was time to go, to say goodbye
to the housekeeper who had found the food for me and looked after me
during the daytime, and goodbye to the Vicaire who had been so busy
on my behalf. He may have been barely 5ft 6in in height, but to me he
would always be 10ft tall.

It was only a few yards along the road to the tram stop, where a few
people were waiting. My guide would get on the vehicle in front of me,
pay the fare for us both and then he would move down the compartment
towards the front exit and I would remain on the back entrance platform.
This plan worked well enough; I could see him and when he was to get
off I would do the same. The tram was full and with frequent stops became

crowded. Very soon half a dozen German soldiers came up the steps
and mingled in so that I was surrounded by them. This was my first close
encounter with the enemy. At the very next stop the crush increased when
an army major joined the throng at my end. He needed room to face
the three officers on the pavement who were attending his departure.
As the tram slowly moved away he stood to attention and stretched his
arm out in the Nazi salute, while the officers seeing him off responded.
It was fortunate neither he nor any of the other ranks standing around
me suspected my true identity. In fact the thought crossed my mind that
they had sudden promotion within their grasp. But their opportunity
disappeared a few more stops later when my guide made a move to
disembark and I followed suit. Another man was waiting in the shadows at the tram stop. I took my raincoat off and gave it to my guide to put
on. The new contact handed me a replacement coat, there was a shaking
of hands, a fleeting goodbye, and my new companion and I walked away
off up the street.

The front walls of the houses were lined up along the back of the pavements; to enter these premises it was only one step across the threshold
from public view to privacy. No. 30 Rue Waroux in Liège had just such
an entrance and, with a light knock on the front door and a step forward,
my companion and I were out of sight of any other pedestrian. We were
greeted by a middle-aged lady who was introduced as Mathilde. My all-
covering raincoat was returned to my companion and with a few brief
words he was gone and I was beckoned forward upstairs. In a small room
I met Mathilde's sister, Jeannie, and another young fellow in civilian
clothes, making me feel rather scruffy in a uniform battledress that
showed the signs of sleeping in the countryside. The young dark-
haired, rather thin, chap said, 'My God, another one', to which I replied,
'It looks like it', and put my hand out saying, 'I am Gordon Mellor', to
which I received his name as Michael Joyce. I do not think that I hesitated
– if I did he did not notice – but the name Joyce struck a chord in my
memory, especially as he had an Irish accent. But because every name
you can think of must have been repeated many times among the tens
of thousands recruited into the RAF, I set aside any doubts that had come
to mind in those introductory seconds. We struck up a friendly relationship straightaway for we would be together for at least several days

whatever future plans were made for us, and mutual support was an attractive thought.

It would seem that Mike had been there for only an hour or so in any case, so Jeannie and Mathilde set about getting us settled in. Two nights running sleeping in a bed was at that time my idea of luxury. In fact we were there for three more nights.

During the following days we had much time to fill in. On the first morning the sisters showed us the escape route off the premises by way of the pair of doors in the back sitting room, up the back garden and through other property owned by their friends, should there be a raid by the German security forces, especially those in the Luftwaffe who had the special responsibility of hunting down fugitive airmen. Our fervent hope was that these doors and the escape route would never need to be used. In the houses in Rue Waroux there must have been at that time a number of families engaged in a constant battle of wits with the men of the occupying armed forces.

Surprisingly, Mike and I did not discuss at length our respective experiences. He did say that he had been on a raid in a Hampden aircraft in August 1940 and on the return journey they had run out of fuel and had force-landed on one of the Dutch islands, the whole crew being made prisoners of war. He also told me that recent events had involved him being sent to work on a farm and on the first night he had been locked up in a bedroom in the roof of the farmhouse, but the farmer had not made sure that the window was secure. During the night hours he had climbed out of the window, slid down the roof to a fairly low level and reached the ground safely to make his escape. He had travelled across country and in the area near Namur had received help, which eventually had transferred him to Liège and so to the home of Jeannie and Mathilde. I must admit I was equally reticent about my own evading history, but it was sufficient for the time and place.

Mike and I received a visit from a tall, rather aged, gaunt lady who to our surprise spoke French with a strong American accent. She was known as Madame Nestor Docteur and despite her name was not of the medical profession. She had been in the American services during the First World War and married a Belgian officer following the Armistice of 1918. It was through her efforts that my uniform was replaced with a grey suit with white pinstripes. My uniform was to be sent back to the Van Meeuwen family. Cloth was very difficult to acquire and there was sufficient there, once washed, to be of use to make clothing for a young boy.

During the first morning here I realised how scruffy I felt and looked. Having no razor I prevailed upon Mike to let me borrow his; this he did readily enough and my appearance improved, which in turn made me feel much better too. This was a fortunate move on my part for a young man arrived carrying a camera, with the intention of taking a photograph of each of us to be used to complete the identity cards being prepared for the next excursion on public transport. He chose a position at the side of the house where there was an entrance closed by a pair of high wooden gates. A non-obtrusive background that was probably repeated many times around the town. A day or two later the photographer was back with the finished documents. Shortly afterwards, that same morning, Madame Docteur also returned with work permits for each of us; I was supposed to be a mechanic named Maurice, but I do not recall the details of Mike's identity. With these documents came the information that we were to move on after lunch that very afternoon. It was a pleasant, warm day with a hint of sunshine, and the anticipation of the new venture added a touch of excitement to our spirits, for we were each on the way forward again.

Shortly after we had finished our midday meal a very smart lady arrived to accompany us on this journey. It was now outlined to Mike and myself that we were to walk away from this house and down to the tram stop to travel to Ans, and then catch a train to Brussels where we would be met. A simple straightforward arrangement it would seem. There was nothing to prepare or pack for – I had nothing other than the suit I was wearing, my identity documents as Maurice and a sum of money for emergencies. Mike appeared to have little more than his razor for shaving. With such delightful weather the absence of overcoats or similar would not cause comment. The tram arrived and we followed the lady on board, but unlike my previous tram ride there were scarcely any other passengers so we sat together. Perhaps this lull in travelling was usual at this time of day and so was used as a precautionary measure. A difficulty was that we had not been given the name of our companion; for security reasons it was not unexpected but it did put a brake on the conversations from time to time. I was to find out that she was known by those in Liège as 'The Dove'. When we arrived at Ans railway station it was deserted to our eyes – nobody in the booking hall, nor on any of the platforms. We had obviously missed the train. There was, of course, someone in the booking office; the three tickets for Brussels were bought and we sat as a small group in the booking hall where we could observe the main entrance and also the doorway on to the platform. I thought time would hang on our hands for there was about an hour to wait, but this was not so. One or two civilians bought tickets and went on the platform to wait. A few soldiers also went through to the platform, to be followed by increasing numbers of others; then officers in field grey uniforms moved purposefully backwards and forwards as if intent on maintaining order and discipline. Time had come for us to join the other passengers waiting on that platform. What a sight that was. There must have been another, well-used, entrance for the platform was packed with uniformed men and women, with a small scattering of local people. The train arrived and, as if by magic, the soldiery all made their way to the reserved coaches in the front of the train and disappeared from view, while the three of us found three empty seats together in a compartment, with four occupied seats opposite us.

As the train for Brussels left Ans station I covertly studied our fellow travellers seated on the opposite side of the compartment. Facing me next to the window was a very plump lady who lost no time in spreading a white cloth over her knees and unwrapping packages of food. In the far corner I found a shortish, rather disagreeable-looking man who was keeping Mike and myself under close scrutiny. I do not think that 'The Dove' escaped his air of distrust either. The couple sitting in between those in the corner seats did not draw attention to themselves and remained aloof. And so we remained, until the lady with the food asked me if I would like some of what she had prepared. This would normally be an opening for a conversation, but my accent would be a direct giveaway. So I gave my version in French of 'No thank you', accompanied by refusal gestures with my hands. Fortunately she did not pursue a dialogue with me and passed on to the other travellers. I did feel uncomfortable by declining her offer for I did not know what the usual behaviour of

Belgians was in these circumstances and we had not been advised on this sort of situation. Such errors could mark you out as being different from everybody else. With a casual air I glanced around, including the man in the far corner, in my view, but not meeting his eyes. My impression was that his sceptical expression had intensified by this event. At home it was not unusual for people to travel for a couple of hours without speaking to others who were travelling. Here we would have to hope that he would take no more notice of us. Fortunately at Leuven, some thirty minutes' journey before Brussels, we left the carriage and its other passengers and took a local train for the rest of the way.

The train ran into Brussels North and we joined the throng of people passing out into the busy life of the capital. Because of the wait at Ans we were later than we should have been and our companion did not see anybody that she recognised in the station precinct. We walked for a while while she explained that she would have to make new arrangements. Leaving us in an adjoining park, she suggested that we walk up and down one of its walkways as many other people were doing, taking the air. This we were able to do, to all intents and purposes a couple of off-duty office workers enjoying the late afternoon's warmth. The walk was well populated with ordinary-looking residents except on one occasion when in the distance Mike and I spotted two huge men approaching. Now my experience of German male physique was limited to a few days, while Mike had been a POW for more than two years and he did not like the appearance of these two men either. What should we do, if anything at all? By agreement we stopped before they reached us, looked at our watches and slowly turned round and walked back the way we had come. We were overtaken, ignored and drew a silent breath of relief when the two broad shoulders went out of a gate in the park railings. I think our imaginations had got the better of our judgement, although according to Mike, German had been the language being spoken by those men.

Our afternoon stroll was soon over and we rejoined 'The Dove' when she reappeared across the road from the park. All was not arranged but she had made progress and had one more call to make. Before long we went down some steps into a below road-level shopping arcade. To me it looked like a smaller version of London's Underground station at Piccadilly Circus, without the escalators but with a series of small shops or kiosks around the perimeter. Again we were left to wait for a few minutes. We were standing in the centre close to a small block of telephone cabins, all in use. Thinking that we wished to use a phone, one of the shop-keepers with an eye to business came across and asked us if we were waiting to make a call, for we could use the one in his shop. This took a bit of getting out of without revealing our origins. With a minimum use of French and more negative hand gestures we survived the encounter.

Satisfactory arrangements now appeared to have been organised, so once more it was off to find a suitable tram route across town. It was hopeless to try and follow the direction that the tram took on this journey for all the streets looked similar, with shops, and all were busy with people. In time our lady rose and got off the tram, to be closely followed by us two; it appeared that our destination was just across the road. Successfully dodging the traffic we approached a house and knocked on a large front door. It was opened by a young girl about seventeen years old, who looked rather startled at being confronted by two strange men. However, her expression changed when our guide revealed herself, to be greeted by 'Oh, hello Aunty' and the door was opened wide to let us in. The young lady was obviously well aware of our situation.

We were led upstairs into a sitting room and introduced to the family of father, mother and three more sisters, all younger than our first acquaintance at the front door. It was difficult to imagine the fortitude of each one, and particularly the two parents who risked everything, including their lives and those of the four daughters, for the courageous ideal of helping their country's allies by aiding us and many others in the same precarious situation. Pleasant as the following hours were in the company of this family, they were soon to be brought to a close; after dark a knock on the front door heralded a serious note to the evening. It was now time for Mike and I to move on in the company of the man who had just arrived. Goodbyes were said to all and we ventured out into the darkness, again to wait for a tram.

As with the afternoon ride it was not possible to identify the route we took or any particular building or even district. Stepping off our transport left us a short walk before we were directed into the entrance hall of an unusual apartment building. Passing into the centre of the building we were confronted with a circular space rising up from the ground to the roof and although there were lifts we took a circular staircase that wound itself up to a projecting gallery at each floor level. The wall at the back of each gallery was punctuated by a series of doors, each one leading to a self-contained flat. At an upper floor our companion produced a set of keys and let us in to an unoccupied apartment. Having closed the door behind us his first words were to say: 'Do not make a noise for there is a Gestapo agent living in the flat next door and sound travels through these walls.' Well, that may have been the truth, or perhaps just a ploy to keep us quiet. Whichever it was neither Mike nor I was going to put the statement to the test. Our natural inclination in the circumstances was to keep out of the public eye as much as possible. Our companion left, saying he would be back in the morning. It is probable that on this day – 15 October – Mike and I were passed over from the Liège-based organisation to 'Comète'.

Mike had first shot at using the bathroom and it was during my turn that our companion of the previous night returned. I was soon dressed except for my jacket, which was being carried as the flat was quite warm; unexpectedly this provoked a situation of some gravity. Until that moment Mike had been answering questions on various matters about his life back in the UK and also on air force matters. He was struggling on some enquiries regarding flying, for being a POW for over two years he was out of date. This time he had been asked: 'What is "Tee Em"?' As a recent publication series I did know of it, but Mike hadn't a clue. I was sitting opposite the other two and our inquisitor shot his first question at me saying, 'Where did you get those braces?' What an odd query, I thought, and naturally looked down – to my horror, on the two brass buckles was impressed the word 'Police'. Now that could raise doubts of anybody's provenance. I explained that I had been to Canada for my flying training and had for part of the time been stationed on a camp run by the Royal Canadian Air Force and it was while there that I had been issued with this pair from RCAF stores and this was the only sort they had in stock at that time. A lot depended on this being accepted, even though it was quite true. The man changed his quizzing to other topics and at last he appeared to be satisfied. But it was quite tricky for a few minutes. If he had still been in doubt my future would have been very uncertain.

Nineteen-year-old Gordon Mellor at his home in Wembley. *All photographs ©Author's Collection.*

'A' Flight, Aberystwyth, February, 1941.

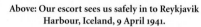

Above: Our escort sees us safely in to Reykjavik Harbour, Iceland, 9 April 1941.

Left: Time for a group picture at Mont Joli, Quebec, 19 April 1941. Gordon in the centre.

Below: Johnny King and Gordon after the first flight at Air Navigation School, RAF Port Albert, Ontario.

Gordon in the cockpit of an Anson.

Above: Burning the
midnight oil before exams.

Left: Waiting for the hot
weather to arrive.

Far left: Leading Aircraftman
Gordon Mellor, Canada, 1941.

Above: Line up of Fairey Battles. Below: Gordon practices air to air firing at No 4 Bombing and Gunnery School, Fingal.

Going home! Departing Canada, October 1941.

Pilots and Navigators of No. 12 Course, RAF Lichfield, November 1941.

Wellington cross country flight.

Gordon on the spar of a Wimpy.

Standing left to right; Eddie Edwards (pilot), George Green (flight engineer), Twiggy Hawthorne (air bomber). Crouched left to right; Norman Macmaster (air gunner), Ginger Richards (air gunner), Gordon Mellor (navigator), Don Macdonald (wireless operator).

Crew of Halifax W 1216 'Q' Queenie. Back row left to right; George Green, Stolz Page, Twiggy Hawthorne, Ginger Richards, Eddie Edwards. Front row left to right; Don Macdonald, Doug Giddens, Norman Macmaster.

10 September 1942. Take off in daylight. Target Dusseldorf.

N
W E
S

FIELDS AND TRACK AT SAME LEVEL — UP HILL
NO BANKS
FARM ACCESS TRACK - BANKS UP ON BOTH SIDES
PAVED ROAD WITH BANKS UP BOTH SIDES
PARACHUTE LANDING IN ORCHARD.
HOUSE SET BACK FROM ROAD
PIELD WITH CABBAGES
REFERRED TO IN STORY ALMOST MET F/SGT. R. HAWTHORN.
FIELDS
DOWN HILL
FARM HOUSE WITH DOG.
DISTANCE NOT KNOWN. BRIGHT FIRE - COULD HEAR AMMUNITION EXPLODING. COULD BE 3 TO 4 KM.
OLD TRENCH OR EXCAVATIONS
X
CRASH SITE ?
ON HIGHER GROUND.

Top: Sketch map of parachute landing in to an orchard.

Above: M. & Mme Van Meeuwen at their front door in Alleur.

Above, right: Carte d'Identitie photograph. Gordon becomes 'Maurice'.

Maurice

Right: Vicair Adons outside his home. Gordon's first night in a bed in the room at top right.

Baron Jean Greindl, 'NEMO'. Head of Comète in Brussels. Arrested February 1943. Executed September 1943.

Above, left: Anne Brusselmans. Comète Helper worked with Michou Dumon. Above, right: No. 37, Rue De Babylon. Home of Robert and Germain Ayle.

Above, left: Robert Ayle, Comète Line Helper. Arrested June 1943. Executed March 1944. Above, right: Germain Ayle. Both Robert and Germain were betrayed by Jean Masson in June 1943.

Andree De Jongh Dédée. Set up the Comète Line with her father in August 1941. Arrested June 1943. Survived. Awarded George Medal.

Above: Elvire De Greef, 'Tante Go'.
Comète organiser in the South of
France. Awarded George Medal.

Above, left: Paul Frederic
De Jongh. Dèdèe's father. Arrested
June 1943. Executed March 1944.

Left: Florentino Goicoechea,
Basque mountain guide.

Daphne.

Bomber Command Observer Gordon Mellor.

The news was that we were off again to another address in Brussels that very morning. I have no recollection of eating breakfast or much else about the flat; my main attention seems to have been directed towards the building, probably in an attempt to remember enough to find it at some time in the future. We set off and again made use of the tramway system. This time, in the morning light, I did pick up a few indications of the route that we were taking. After leaving the tram I recall crossing a wide boulevard with a division down the centre of the roadway – separating the two directions of the flow of traffic – then going up two or three stone steps into a most attractive house where we were taken upstairs to the rooms close under the roof. While not being told who our host was by name, we did find out that she originally came from Luxembourg and that the man and wife team who looked after her were also of the same nationality.

With the frequent comings and goings in the house, the two of us were restricted to the rooms on the top floor. There was extra furniture there in store but we were comfortable enough. Under these conditions it was difficult to remember that we were 'on the run' in an occupied country, where food was rationed and in short supply as well. No doubt some of what we ate was from the black market. The unease that we felt was probably due to the fact that both Mike and myself had been in the open air night and day, walking through the countryside and making our own decisions. Now we had to follow other people's instructions and were dependent upon them for our safety. In addition, during the previous twenty-four hours we had made six or seven journeys on public transport, which had required us to merge in with the crowd, to be watchful without constantly looking over our shoulders and to avoid attracting any attention from other travellers or German military or security personnel. To do so would be a disaster and undo all that had already been achieved. It could also expose any helper who was close to us and commit them to the firing squad.

During the succeeding days we were given advice by a new figure on the scene, again no names were mentioned, which was understandable but very frustrating. We were advised not to attempt to speak French under any circumstances; I hadn't thought that my pronunciation was that bad, but apparently it was. Then word was brought that we were to move on early the next morning. That same evening the lady of the house invited Mike and myself to join her for the evening meal, a most generous and pleasant experience. A particular moment to be recalled many times afterwards was hearing the BBC radio news broadcast after the meal and learning about the situation in North Africa. Listening to British radio was forbidden by the occupying German forces, and reacting against this order was to me a simple act of defiance at a time when there was little else that one could do.

Not knowing the identity of some of the helpers at the time of first contact was quite disconcerting, for I was becoming increasingly indebted to so many unknown people. How would I ever trace them after the war was over to convey my heartfelt thanks? Generally in 1942 there was no thought of a peace agreement; much had to change before an invasion could be contemplated and in many units of the armed forces it was largely a question of living from day to day. Despite the commonly held belief that 'It won't happen to me', in the squadrons of Bomber Command it frequently did. But for many years the identities of these contacts remained unresolved. Gradually over the years information became available by personal contacts, exchange visits, the publication of books and the release of former reports and papers from the national records. So now I can say that my contact in the Liège area came about by a combination of at least two groups: Service Zero and JAM. The linking name was Mr Louis Rademecker, and his many colleagues included Mr Paul Balteau and Mademoiselle Gertrude Moors, who died at Ravensbrück concentration camp in May 1945. The person we knew as 'The Dove' was Therese Grandjean, also known by many other names. The family Mike and I stayed with on arrival in Brussels was that of Dr Antoine Goethals. We also had contact with a man named Guerry and with Baron Albert Greindl, brother of the 'Nemo' leader of Comète in Brussels at that time.

Mike and I were up early in the morning and were ready to start the journey when our usual visitor arrived to accompany us. We had already expressed our gratitude to the lady of the house for having us there and also said our goodbyes the previous evening, for we would not see her the following day. We stepped out into the half light, walked downhill and through the still sleepy streets to join other early travellers at the Gare du Midi. Spreading out we passed on to the platform and found our places on the train now waiting to depart. Tickets and documents were in order and we settled down on this initial stage with Lille in France as our first objective. I tried to appear as casual and alike as those others travelling, but I cannot say that my thoughts matched my outward demeanour, for there was the matter of making the border crossing not all that far away.

Eventually the train slowed and stopped altogether, for the passengers to be greeted by shouts from the staff lining the platform requiring everybody to get off the train. This we did, with some trepidation. There was a large number of people all heading the same way, towards some low buildings. Our companion set off, leaving Mike to follow well behind and then myself way to the rear. If either of us were to be confronted with a problem then the other two would not be affected. I assumed that there had been no trouble as many people had already passed through and there was nobody in view who I recognised. There were two rooms to negotiate; papers were looked at first and then we shuffled forward into the next room, occupied by a long bench with customs officers behind, examining baggage. Ominously two armed German soldiers stood on the travellers' side watching the proceedings. My turn came and I placed my small attaché case in front of the customs officer. As I moved to open it he asked me a question; I hadn't a clue what it was that he had said. Think quickly – it probably was, 'Have you anything to declare?' I shrugged my shoulders and spread my hands to imply that I had nothing and adopted a suitable expression of negation on my face. I could mentally feel that armed soldier's gun pointing straight at my back. This was the crunch moment, had I guessed correctly? The customs inspector chalked a mark on the case, nodded his head and I picked up the case and walked out on to the platform, free to get on the train that had pulled through across the border with only the train staff on board. Suddenly the sunshine felt just that bit warmer on the French side. I now gladly joined my companions in the carriage for the remaining miles into Lille.

Gordon's metro ticket for his 'tour' of Paris with Robert Ayle.

Chapter 7

Tour de France

There was just over an hour to wait at Lille for our next train. Hanging about on the station concourse with the probability of security people watching from the sidelines did not seem to be a good idea, so we went across the road to the cafe conveniently placed to keep the station in sight. Three coffees and a couple of newspapers helped us to give an authentic appearance. I have to say that Mike and I had difficulty in presenting a convincing representation of intelligent readers; we exchanged our halves of one of the papers too often, should anybody have noticed. Eventually the hour or so passed and it was back on to the platform for the train to Paris. While awaiting its arrival I looked along the platform and saw two figures that stood out from the crowd – everything about them was contrary to the appearance of the Belgian people. I mentioned this to our companion and was surprised to hear him say that they were travelling in the same way as ourselves. We were to know them later as Alexis and Petro, two Russian aviators who were escaped prisoners of war. My reaction to the news was to wonder if in our own way Mike and I also stood out from the local people and were equally conspicuous. With the general bustle of boarding the train I lost sight of the two Russian airmen.

The railway journey to the Paris terminal was completed without incident and arrival there only required us to follow our escort at a distance. The crowd of passengers streamed off the platform, with us practically submerged in the crush at the gates at the rail-head but fortunately creating little interest from the German military, which seemed to have a substantial presence on the main concourse. We were being led towards a small group of people waiting, as were many others. Greetings and handshakes were brief and we were soon descending the stairs to the Metro. During this short period I was asked by our journey companion as to whether I had any money. Of course I had and I could see that the Belgian and Dutch currency would be of help towards the costs of our travel; I passed all the notes that I had for those two countries to him and as soon as we reached the bottom of the stairs he nodded to us and slipped away from our view.

Our first journey in Paris started with passing through the Metro barrier down on to the platform with a gentleman wearing round glasses, brushed-back grey hair and probably in his upper fifties, who appeared to be the leader of the little group and answered to the name of Paul. One of his colleagues fulfilled perfectly my imaginary vision of a typical Parisian: suave, smooth black hair and a thin line moustache on the upper lip; he was dressed in a very nice dark suit and was introduced as Robert Aylé. The third man of the party was much younger than the other two and attached himself to Mike, resulting in my not having a good memory of his appearance. After a trip requiring two, maybe three, changes we all disembarked and left the Metro by means of stairs and an exit at street level surrounded by ornamental ironwork displaying the name Sevres Babylone. This was the parting of the ways, with the assurance that we would meet again. Mike left with his younger French helper. Paul went off on his own and I accompanied Robert Aylé along the rue de Babylone. We crossed the road and soon reached No. 37, with a large window open on to the pavement and occupied by a woman concierge who controlled the comings and goings of people using the building. Robert nodded to her and not only did she return the nod but also looked straight at me; my reaction was to think 'She will know me again for sure' before being let in through the front door. Passing along a wide entrance passage it opened out into an open-air courtyard with stairs and galleries to each floor. Of course we had to climb to the very top flat where I was welcomed by Madame Germaine Aylé.

The flat was quite small, but ideal for Robert and Germaine in normal times, and consisted of a sitting room with a large window, a kitchen, a bathroom and one bedroom. But, these were not normal times, far removed indeed, leaving the question of where I was to sleep unanswered for the time being. After the evening meal there was a knock on the door and Germaine let in a visitor who introduced herself in English with rather a strong Irish accent. She had summed me up quickly enough and was used to finding strange young men in residence here. I now found out that her role was as a teacher as well as a friend. Consequently, for the next hour I was involved in their weekly English lesson. The incongruity of this particular situation was not lost on the small company gathered there that evening. The visitor departed for home and my sleeping arrangements became clear. In addition to the table and chairs that we had been using during the evening, the sitting room also contained a decorative, firmly upholstered French sofa with arms at each end limiting the length of its seat. With blankets to hand I assured them that I would be comfortable. The sitting room became my bedroom.

Being over 6ft in height I was soon to find that the sofa and I were not compatible, for the seat was much too short and the ends, although padded, would not let me stretch out. With my head on a pillow, my feet and the lower part of my legs were left dangling in mid-air and with the reverse posture my head was unsupported. By midnight I knew that I had bones and muscles that I had not realised existed before. In the morning at breakfast I had to confirm that I had slept well. In the circumstances, what else could one do; I did not wish to appear ungrateful.

Plans had already been made for me to go and get a photograph taken – to affix to a new set of documents allowing me to travel and also to declare my occupation – so all I had to do was wait for the appearance of the man who would accompany me. In the meantime, I sat near the open window and made myself familiar with the position of the many landmarks in view. During this time M. Aylé had a visitor, a rather elderly, heavily built man of business. He bid me good morning in French to which I replied and, as he did not make any further attempts at conversation, I kept quiet. His discussion with Robert was soon over. I did wonder what the visitor thought of me; probably he was well aware of the clandestine business that was being carried on from this apartment, for I had not been asked to go into another room out of sight.

At last a youngish man, who I had not met before, arrived and explained what we were going to do. This was a useful practice for it prepared one for the coming event. So off the two of us went down the stairs and out into the rue de Babylone, acknowledging the concierge as we passed her window. It was our intention to go to one of the principal stations and I seem to remember that it was the Gare de L'Est, where we found a kiosk that took and processed photographic portraits suitable for identity cards and the like. I handed over the correct sum of francs, sat in the booth, waited for the flash to fire, and that was it for the time being. The machine was in continual use and we went away for half an hour while the processing was completed. After the appropriate time had expired we went back and the attendant recognised me. He put the finished photo in an envelope and handed it to me without a word. I nodded my thanks and off we went back by Metro to rue de Babylone. It was easy, it all went according to plan, but even in that short expedition of less than two hours there was a dozen occasions when it could have gone wrong. I was constantly ensuring that I did not draw attention to myself – perhaps that in itself was a giveaway. Paris was a busy city, more so to me than Brussels, and being so seemed more threatening. I was learning fast.

The afternoon brought further unexpected happenings. Robert and I went out again and on leaving the building we turned left and walked along the rue de Babylone until the rue Vaneau was encountered. When a particular house number was reached, Robert led the way up to what I think was a second-floor apartment; it could have been the third floor, I am not sure now. However, on following Robert into the flat I was greeted by the occupant – a most attractive Frenchwoman named Elizabeth Barbier – and then introduced to a young man about my own age by the name of Lorne Kropf, a Canadian pilot officer also hoping to return to England. Barely had we made ourselves known to each other when there was a further knock on the door. The next arrival was Mike Joyce, so it was introductions all round once again. Robert and his colleague left and Elizabeth and the three aviators were soon exchanging experiences, information and confidences as if we were old friends. During this time Mike and I brought each other up to date and Lorne gave us a run-down on Kitchener, his home town in Ontario, Canada, and a town I had visited myself while over there a year previously. Night had already fallen before we left to return to the rue de Babylone, leaving Lorne Kropf in situ.

Robert was very proud of Paris, his home town, and sensing my interest he seized the opportunity one afternoon to suggest that we take a walk together. The idea appealed to me as I was feeling the lack of fresh air and exercise and it was warm, sunny and inviting. He led the way and I was eager to see all that was available. Before long the busy roads gave way to a wide approach and we were then facing Les Invalides, dominated by its huge dome. The building was busy with visitors; we mingled with them and from above viewed Napoleon's tomb in the chamber below. The walk continued as if everything was normal, we were just two people seeing the sights as indeed were many people. Were we really at war? Way up in front of us stood the Eiffel Tower; this was bound to be popular but strangely enough it was not. I soon found out the reason why not for Robert explained that only German occupying forces were allowed entrance to the structure. While there were a fair number of off-duty military at ground level, one couldn't judge how many were aloft.

Affecting only a passing interest, as if familiar with the scene, we continued across the bridge spanning the Seine and about halfway across we were accosted by a priest, who it turned out was well known to Robert. I was swiftly introduced to the cleric, who shook hands and greeted me in my own language and explained that he was from the cathedral of Notre Dame where Robert and Germaine were parishioners. The conversation continued for a few minutes in a mixture of French and English and then we parted, going opposite ways. Robert and I headed directly towards the Arc de Triomphe at the end of the road. Again, this was a popular meeting place for the occupying military forces. To approach the arch itself would have attracted attention, for I could not pick out any civilians on the centre island among the many uniforms. Our direction changed to take us down the Avenue des Champs-Élysées and shortly afterwards, marching towards us, there was a German military band followed by a long column of field-grey soldiers. The band commenced playing martial music, so that they entered the area around the arch in ceremonial fashion. This was obviously a propaganda set piece intended to impress the local population of their strength as the occupying force. Yes, we certainly were at war. I was now considering whether our walk was entirely innocent, for very many French people were deeply offended by the presence of the Germans and their harsh authority. Was this an act of defiance on Robert's part? For he and his wife were already most active in helping fallen Allied airmen to return to England to rejoin the fight against Germany. It was a major activity, dangerous in the extreme, and attracted the most serious of penalties.

During this stage of the walk, having continued with the air of not wanting to be seen to be looking at the troops, I noticed that there was a shortage of taxis. They had, however, been replaced by what I can best describe as bicycle rickshaws. They had side-by-side seating for two passengers at the back of a tricycle frame, while the driver sat in front and controlled the steering as well as provided the leg power. They appeared to be in demand. The walk progressed until a suitable crossing of the Seine became available and the last stage down to the rue de Babylone brought us back to No. 37 and a welcome rest. It was only in the latter part of the walk that I really felt uncomfortable for I was already aware that from time to time the security forces would block off both ends of a road and examine everybody's documents. If yours were not satisfactory there was a problem; also young men could be detained and sent off to labour camps to work for the state. It was simply a case of being in the wrong place at the wrong time. I wasn't supposed to be there in any case. The wide streets and boulevards and open areas were not an issue; it was in the narrow streets with no side turnings that could see this sort of impromptu exercise commence, with no escape route.

I saw Elizabeth Barbier perhaps twice more, in much the same situation as the first rendezvous in her flat. Lorne Kropf was still there and Mike also joined us. During these meetings it was made known to us that Elizabeth was engaged in a double game; indeed, she was an active member of the movement that Mike and I had transferred into, but also she had formed a liaison with a senior German officer of the security forces and was able from this source to pass back any relevant information that she overheard. This was a most dangerous situation, but she was not the only one to be successful in this duplicity. Word was passed to us that Mike, Lorne and I were to make the next journey forward together; also one other would join the party. It was not long before we were to find out who. Goodbyes had been said to Germaine, and with Robert I left the flat at the top of the building and we set off for the mainline station to head for the south. The meeting at that station was a low-key affair, punctuated by handshakes on the arrival of each of the travellers. There were the three of us as predicted; the fourth proved to be Alexis Stadnik, a sergeant in the Russian Air Force and one of the two Russians who we had seen previously on the platform at Lille railway station. Our companions who had brought each of us to the station disappeared one by one, leaving us in the charge of a young lady who had emerged from the shadows and another man. The lady was Andrée de Jongh, known as 'Dédée' who had conceived and created the Comète Ligne d'evasion with Arnold Deppé and her father 'Paul'. As for the extra man there was some doubt, but I have seen a report that suggests that it probably was 'Franco', Jean-François Nothomb. The six of us boarded the train into what appeared to be a reserved compartment seating just that number and no room for an unknown traveller. It was very dark outside and the compartment lights were quite dim. The railway journey commenced.

Apart from the checks for tickets and papers we were left alone. My identity had been changed from that used in Belgium. I was travelling in the name of Jean Petit, a mechanic, and I now had occasion to ponder as to whether somebody had a sense of humour in giving me that name for I was at that time some 6ft 2in tall. The other matter to come to mind was the comparison of my present progress overnight in a fast passenger train and my situation following jumping from the plane; then my movement had been secretive and slow – how far would I have travelled by now? Much would have depended on my ability to find food and drink. I was still heading for the same destination as my original decision, but there was a tiny, irksome feeling of losing control. Overall there was not the slightest doubt that these people accompanying us on the train really knew what they were doing, for their organisation was superb.

Morning came, with the travellers' usual unwillingness to greet the new day; already the sun was bright and quite warm and by mid-morning the train was slowing down to crawl into Bayonne station. This was to be our only change, for the next stage was by use of a local train. During the waiting time Dédée said the next train could be crowded and not to stand as a group but to separate a little, and that on arrival at Saint-Jean-de-Luz there would be people to meet us. We were each to follow their instructions as we would all be leaving that station independently and making our way to the next address by different routes and timings.

The local train pulled in and sure enough it was packed with people. With much pushing I squeezed into the corridor. Passengers were standing, even in the compartments, so there was no chance of a seat. I caught a glimpse of Mike a few yards down the corridor yet was unable even to turn around. During the journey a ticket inspector tried to do his job, but he got no assistance from the passengers; after all it was a Sunday and a day to spend by the sea. Glimpses of the sun shining on the water had been caught briefly from the train windows.

At Saint-Jean-de-Luz, everybody wanted to get off at once. Until now, every time the train had veered round a bend we'd had to hang on, not that there had been any fear of falling over in that squash of people. But now the doors were opened the passengers popped out like champagne corks. I followed the flow; that was all one could do. Even at this point we were still within occupied France, the German forces having retained control of the coastal area right down to the border with Spain. I looked up and down the platform for the members of our party; meaningful looks flashed between Dédée and others. Soon order was formed from apparent chaos and we four evaders left the station separately and outside were met and greeted with handshakes and introductions to local people waiting for us. In pairs we slipped away from the station to disappear into the busy streets. My partner was 'B' Johnson and instead of making a direct walk to our resting place we strolled down towards the harbour and sat on a bench seat for a chat until it was time for us to join the others at the home of another Comète helper.

It was only a short walk from the harbour area for 'B' Johnson and myself to reach the building where we would rejoin the others. We approached a door between the shops to the upper apartments and found that we were the last to arrive; my fellow travellers had already settled themselves in with the family, who I also found to be very welcoming. During the day we had several talks and here we were helped unexpectedly by Mike, who managed with some Polish to draw Alexis into the conversations; apparently there were similarities with Russian and Polish. It was revealed that Alexis and Petro, both aviators, had escaped from a prison camp not all that far from Berlin. This was the first time that Mike had revealed that he had associated with the Poles – was it in their country from which he had escaped from the farm? It didn't quite tie up. We stayed the night and were glad to get a good sleep, for tomorrow was to be another day of physical exertion and progress.

By early afternoon the four of us were ready to tackle the next stage and we had the pleasure of two young ladies calling for us. One of them was Janine, daughter of Elvire de Greef known as 'Tante Go' the chief in the south of France. The other girl was still a mystery, for others were also engaged in this enterprise. We ventured forth into the street below to find that our new companions had a bicycle each, which they just pushed at first. We followed towards the harbour and then over the road bridge, crossing the river and looking very much as a young mixed group out for an afternoon of leisure; well we hoped we looked as innocent as that. Our steps took us on to a road running out of town into the country-side. Progress that balmy afternoon was unhurried and the walking was punctuated by the occasional ride on one of the bicycles. The route along the dusty road bypassed the town of Urrugne on a hill away to our right as we slowly mounted the slope towards a farmstead at Bidegain Berri.

Traffic had not been a problem for it had virtually been non-existent but, even so, one was not sorry when – rounding that last easy bend in the road – one of the girls pointed out to us our destination, a farmhouse sitting there on the very edge of the stony road. We approached it at the same pace that we had used all afternoon; although there were other properties in view it was unlikely any resident would comment on seeing visitors call at the farm. The main entrance door was in the flank wall of the square building that looked as if it was capable of withstanding all weathers. We had been under observation from the house, for as we arrived at the door it was opened by Frantxia Uzandizanga and we were ushered into a central hallway that stretched like a corridor through the house to the far end. On the right-hand side one could hear the breathing noises of animals. Sure enough, Frantxia opened a wide wooden door to reveal the cow byre. The other side of the corridor held the living quarters of the house and there four rather tired airmen gratefully sat down. The two girls seemed to be quite unaffected by the afternoon's exercise and soon disappeared to return to Saint-Jean-de-Luz on their bicycles. With some food and a refreshing drink, vigour returned to each of us left behind.

Gradually the afternoon light began to fade, as we passed the time talking between ourselves and with Frantxia, who ran the farm herself and had two children of which there was no sign at this time. This southern part of occupied France was heavily guarded in view of the proximity of the border with Spain and our little group had been very fortunate not to encounter any of the many patrols during the afternoon walk to Bidegain-Berri. Even with the most meticulous planning there was always the chance that the unexpected event could ruin all that had been achieved. For myself, I felt during the past weeks that I had had more than one person's share of good fortune; sitting there I could only hope that there would be no change. Having walked all afternoon towards those peaks on the skyline that we should be crossing that night, to fall at this decisive stage could not be contemplated.

Suddenly and almost without a sound, Dédée was with us again, joined only minutes later by Florentino, a giant of a man who seemed to fill the room. He was a Spanish Basque with an outstanding knowledge of both French and Spanish sides of the border country. Preparations for the night were put in hand, shoes were put into a haversack and were replaced with espadrilles tied on with laces that were inspected by Florentino to make sure they would not slip off. To travel over rough ground with perhaps only one foot protected would be a danger not only to oneself but also to everyone else. None of the escapers had much more than the clothes they stood up in.

Instructions were brief: follow Florentino closely in single file; do not lag behind; do exactly as he instructs at once; do not make any noise or talk, for sound travels a long way at night; and do not smoke. Not that any of us did as far as I can remember. Even though all this was common sense it did no harm to spell it out. The route to be pursued was briefly described to us as a walk over rough country, gaining height as we went along until we reached a steep valley with a river at the bottom; the centre of this was the border to Spain. We would wade across the river – providing it was possible to do so – climb up the bank to cross a railway line and a patrolled road, then head up that side of the valley. On reaching the top it was intended to negotiate rough country downwards to our destination. The only other matter was in which order we were to walk behind Florentino. I was to be at the back, with Dédée just in front of me.

As soon as daylight had faded away we made our goodbyes and gave our thanks to Frantxia. After waiting for a few minutes in the darkened hallway for our eyes to adapt to the reduced light we slipped out of the door by which we had entered. Despite our precautions, after the brightness of the sitting room the night seemed dense black. A few strides down the road we stepped off into a meadow; almost immediately our guide stopped and gave each of us a stout stave cut beforehand from a thicket for use on the uneven ground ahead. Now eyes were getting used to the night and the solid blackness seemed to lift a little. Was everybody in their correct position in the line? Then it was time to set off.

The route crossed varied farmland, with the occasional wet spot where the mud tried to pull your espadrilles from your feet if you wandered a pace or two off Florentino's track. The ground underfoot gradually gave way to harder, stony slopes and the incline increased to a crest where the strain on the legs eased for a while. But this was followed by another slope to be overcome and another ridge to cross, always gaining height as well as progressing forward. At some points we had the benefit of woodland to cover our movements and, surprisingly, also high green slopes where flocks of sheep were still grazing. While this made walking more comfortable for a time and reduced the noise of our footsteps, it could have revealed our presence to a patrol of border guards. Many of the sheep had bells on collars around their necks; as the flock moved away from our approach the resulting jingle increased greatly. The disturbance could easily have given away our position.

The stars had been bright for the early hours of the trek but were now dimmed with the brilliance of the large and circular rising moon. The landscape became bathed in light and it was apparent that Florentino was still concerned we might yet be discovered, and urged us to put on speed to reach less revealing stretches of our route. Far to the right of us we had glimpsed the faint lights of the Spanish coastal towns; perhaps even as far as San Sebastian and the lighthouse at Fuenterrabia. Our instructions were to keep up with Florentino and to keep quiet, but our guide was a man of iron and maintaining his pace had been difficult and left no breath for talking. And not only was he carrying a substantial rucksack but he also had a large black metal box on his shoulders.

As we climbed higher the whole landscape began to spread out around us; the moonlight flooded across the southern slopes and left dark shadows elsewhere. Our guide was still troubled by the amount of light and with cautionary whispers to be as quiet as possible the party hurried onwards, stopping only occasionally to rest legs and to ease the shortness of breath. Eventually the walking became less arduous and one of our premier objectives appeared in front of us, below. The ground fell away steeply into a deep shadowed valley down to the River Bidassoa, with many trees lining the slopes on each side of the watercourse. There was the border, which marked the limits of occupied France. Descending taxed the leg muscles severely, as did the many slips and stumbles amid the bushes and saplings covering the lower slopes; it took a long time and much effort to reach the narrow terrace of meadow that led to the riverbank. The immediate approach to the waterway was obscured by many trees and bushes, but there with some reflection from the sky was a major obstacle – the river itself. Passage across had to be made here as the water rushed over the rock-strewn bed; there was at this time no other fordable point close by.

Trousers were stripped off and bundled up to be carried above the level of the water. After a brief show of rather pale legs the group lowered themselves down the bank into the water, which reached to a little over knee height. Florentino headed towards the opposite bank, which seemed to be quite remote. With a wave of his arm to indicate that the crossing was fordable I started to make my way over using my stave as a balancing leg, for the bottom of the river seemed to be covered with large, flat, smooth stones. The depth of the water increased towards the middle so that it rose to about hip level; with each step the pressure of the current increased, threatening to break my foothold and brush me aside and away. The far side was in shadow but I felt the weight of the flow ease as the water shallowed – the bank was within my grasp. Safe above the cold water I was glad to get my trousers back on and joined the others for the next section that had to be overcome.

At a higher level through the trees and bushes was the railway line and beyond that, even further up, was the road, subject to patrol by guards from time to time. So, upwards and onwards in silence through the trees and undergrowth, with no train to be heard as we reached the track. Next it was up to the road, with Florentino crashing branches with the large black box on his shoulders. So much for us keeping quiet. A careful look in both directions along the road was taken before we proceeded.

To the left could be seen the customs building with its lights showing quite brightly; to the right there was nothing in view for it was in shadow. Opposite our position the valley side ran up steeply from the road edge. Florentino was the first over into the darkness on the far side, while Dédée stayed to give the signal to each one when to make his dash across the highway. We had been warned that close to the crossing point there was a large and quite deep pit to be avoided.

It was then a case of grasping tufts of coarse grass and anything else available in order to climb on hands, feet and knees up the steep valley side and to continue up to the top without stopping. It was not until we had all gathered together at a high point, with heaving chests – and that Florentino had come to a halt and reached into a bush to produce a bottle of brandy to pass around – that we grasped the fact that we now stood on Spanish soil and that German-controlled occupied France was away over there on the other side of the valley. It was a great and unexpectedly emotional moment. We savoured it for a minute or two, Mike and I shook hands, and then it was off on our way again. There was still the Spanish patrols to avoid, and if arrested the consequent internment, probably in Miranda prison camp, of ill repute, away to the south. Time pressed for there was still a long way to go and we must not be caught on the open mountainside in daylight.

When moving off we had fallen into line in the same order as previously; once again we were crossing upper slopes with shadowy areas that must have hidden us from view now and again until we reached the top where we were in full moonlight once more. Not a place to stay too long. The pattern of the terrain rising to a high point and then falling again continued, but I felt that we were in fact losing height. Progress did improve when we reached a wide track of coarse stone, probably used by the military patrols with vehicles. For us in light footwear of espadrilles the surface was not very kind to feet already tired; however, it was easier than some of the ground we had already encountered. The moonlight was fading and there was more vegetation now to give us some cover on the lower slopes. Looking downwards we could see small patches of mist forming. Much encouragement was forthcoming from Dédée, and from Florentino often in the form of 'dos cien metros'.

It was daylight and the mist was thick. The temperature had dropped for it was markedly colder, and after some steep tracks down we were on fairly level ground on well-marked paths and a paved roadway passing the occasional building. But despite Florentino's encouragement the miles seemed endless. The pace slowed and then there looming out of the fog was some kind of structure. It looked like a farmhouse with the end wall facing the road, and we walked round the corner on to a paved front yard. We had reached our destination and eagerly made for the front door. Inside was a large room with a wooden table and long wooden seats on each side. Adjoining this room was a big, warm kitchen. Sinking on to chairs with relief, we soon welcomed a hot breakfast. Has food before or since ever tasted so good?

Then Dédée and Florentino made preparations to move on and were quick to say their farewells, for there was much for them to do before they retraced their steps back to Saint-Jean-de-Luz. Would the rest of us have faced the rigours of that journey again so soon, or had their dedication? They were both to repeat that double crossing many times. I felt that we would not see their equal ever again.

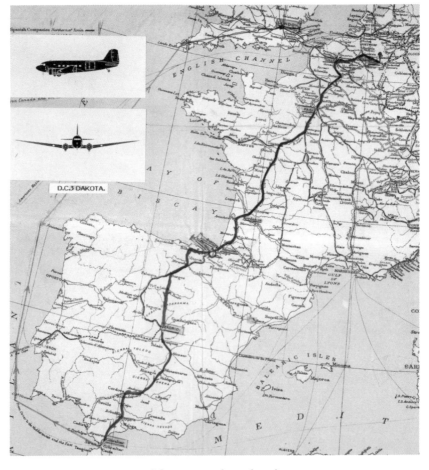

'A long way round to get home.'

Chapter 8

Birthday Present

At the safe house the welcome, the warm food and the comforting temperature of the vast kitchen combined with the release of tension – that
had swept us over all obstacles on the rough trail overnight for some 40
kilometres – left me with a previously unknown depth of fatigue. The
long, narrow wooden form drew me like a magnet and I lay down on it
as if on a feather bed. I slept, perched on this narrow ledge, until some
time later a hard shove on the shoulder brought me wide awake. There
must have been a residual awareness somewhere in my thoughts that
we had to move on once again.

The car to transport us into San Sebastian had arrived. There was
one more parting, this time with those here who had so willingly given
us food and shelter to help us on our way. We crammed ourselves in with
Bernardo Aracama, the driver of the car – three on the rear seat and one
in the front next to our new helper; I still have the feeling that I was the
lucky one in front. It was a small car so our progress was more majestic
than fast. I only recall a long, straight tree-lined town road – no other detail
remains – until the car came to a halt in an area with buildings at the
back of the narrow pavements on both sides. It was full daylight but our
instructions were simple: to get out of the car one by one, cross the road
purposefully and walk straight through the doorway our guide indicated
and up the stairs inside to the flat above. Nobody seemed to take any
notice, despite other figures crossing the road and going in the same
doorway. Bernardo's wife and young son Claudio were there to greet us.
While Bernardo had been away collecting the four of us, his wife had
been busy preparing food pending our arrival. A quick wash to freshen
up and then we gathered around to join the family for the meal. Despite

the mixture of languages the conversation flowed, with the help of many gestures and facial expressions; even Alexis Stadnik relaxed and made his particular contribution. Afterwards the four of us congregated in the bedroom, with a quick toss of coins to decide the choice of bed before crashing down into oblivion for a few hours.

Much later we were visited by a young man from the British consulate, which I understood to be in Bilbao. He collected basic information of identity and also revealed that arrangements were being made on our behalf. Our part was to be ready to travel the next day. We had been ready for weeks to travel at any time, for we had nothing more than the clothes we stood up in and what was in our pockets – did he think we had luggage? Ah well, he was a nice, friendly young man and he was doing his best for us so we did not press the point.

We must have looked as if we were starving refugees, for another repast was prepared by the Aracamas, with us as their guests. The meal was mainly fish of course, as we were so close to the sea, but varieties unusual to the British table. To be sure, the hospitality of Bernardo and his family was exceptional, for not only had he known us for just a few hours, but was acting contrary to the official government response to the arrival of escaping airmen into Spanish territory. Even here, in a professed neutral country, there were harsh penalties to be endured if the authorities became aware of such activities.

Next day there were more partings following the arrival of the young Englishman with a car. Saying goodbye became more difficult each time, despite the briefness of the encounter, for I could not but feel that my share of good fortune in knowing such dedicated people should have run out before now. But here we were, off down the stairs and into a large vehicle with an official driver awaiting us at the kerbside. There was plenty of room for everyone; a brief wave and then we were on our way.

'Where are we going?'

'Oh, to Madrid of course.' That was over 250 miles – a giant leap forward.

Having left town the driver put the car into top gear and I felt sure he didn't change gear all the way. When we came to hills he just put his foot down on the accelerator for more power and we surged up as if the hill wasn't there. On the road to Burgos we swept past the notorious detention camp of Miranda de Ebro, a vast enclosed area of wooden huts.

The very destination that would have been for us if we had been inter-cepted by the Spanish border guards after crossing the River Bidassoa. We were there now, but thankfully on the outside looking in.

With the small Union Jack on the bonnet of the car streaming in the breeze, there was no attempt to hide the identity of those inside; all I could think was that there was some form of diplomatic immunity pro-tecting the occupants, which was a vast improvement in our status, achieved merely by getting into a particular automobile. An occasional duo of police-men closely watched the vehicle as it passed through small communities, but no more than that. Once or twice progress was restricted by a flock of sheep being driven along the road in search of new pasture; it was explained to us that the shepherd's total worldly wealth was tied up in his flock and that ultimately he would head for a market to convert the sheep into money, only to start again with a new flock and range over the countryside for months at a time.

After dark the rural country scene disappeared, to be replaced by suburbs and city streets. Then, unexpectedly, we were suddenly facing a large pair of wooden gates, which were swung open for us – we had arrived at the British Embassy in Madrid. It was a relief to get out of the car and stretch our legs. The accommodation offered to us was in a large room with many beds, followed by an introduction to a large group of men of many nations from all over Europe who greeted us in a dozen or more languages. In no time we were one of them, and if anything our rather mixed clothing was in better condition than their own. Every one had been 'on the run', hoping to get to England and join in the conflict to free their home countries. In the meantime they stayed within the embassy until they could be moved on to the next stage of their journey, as we did ourselves.

The next morning we four evaders were interviewed by the air attaché, who was mainly interested in noting the names, service numbers and details of identity of each one of us. I do not know what he made of our Russian companion and Alexis was not forthcoming either. After that, the day was regulated by mealtimes, and the intervening hours were of a social nature with much discussion on experiences in getting to this temporary home. Playing card games and visits by various Spanish itinerant salesmen – who supplied razor blades, soap, combs and a vast selection of minor necessities all for a few pesetas each – were other alternative time fillers. After the evening meal the night seemed to be set aside for taking part in an international form of poker; despite the variety of language everybody understood the complexity of play amid considerable good humour. For an hour or two they could forget their particular problems and the heartache that was always there and never far from the surface of their thoughts.

Soon news of our impending departure was common knowledge and the object of some curiosity, for being the last to arrive we were now going to be the first to move on. Strangely enough we were not progressing under our own names but with others that were given to us by an official at the embassy. I was to travel under the title of Captain Randle. I have no recollection of the monikers given to my companions, but many years later I learned that an evader, RAF pilot Sergeant William Randle and captain of a Wellington aircraft of 150 Squadron, had passed through Comète and the embassy just three weeks previously. Was it just coincidence or part of a deliberate policy that names were exchanged and was my own name so used by a subsequent evader or escaper at a later date? If so, I have never been aware of this taking place.

We departed from the embassy with a little more than we had on arrival, for I had acquired a razor, shaving brush, soap and towel during my stay. Passing through the large entrance gates into the busy city streets was low key, as was the entry a day or two before. This time we were accompanied by a young member of staff who led us to a busy restaurant for a substantial meal, then off to the main railway station to ensure that we were established in the seats reserved for the four of us. The instructions were to stay in the compartment and seats provided until the train arrived at the station most suitable for passing into Gibraltar, where further advice would be available. The final gesture was to hand over several bottles of red wine and with a handshake he was gone. And soon we were off too. It did not take long to establish that there were no catering facilities on the train, hence the restaurant meal that we had enjoyed during the evening. It was going to be a protracted night, so we opened a bottle of wine and sampled it. The taste was rough – very rough – and coarse, like liquid sandpaper on the throat. My interest died immediately; someone made the comment that 'it would put hairs on your chest'. My anatomy satisfied me as it was, so I resolved to try to sleep.

Morning came and with it aching limbs and a cold, shivery consciousness. From now on at intervals the train stopped at intermediate stations and with the morning sun came some welcome warmth. In addition there were also vendors selling water, a variety of snacks and rather fatty-looking cooked foods, none of which I ventured to buy.

In the early afternoon the steady progress of the train slowed and at long last crawled into the station at which we were required to get off. Sure enough, we were directed to get on to a mini coach and were soon passing through La Línea and approaching the departure point from Spain. Up ahead was a large, flat open landscape with barely any significant feature to focus on, but beyond was a different matter altogether, for there it stood, that vast vertical face of the Rock. This was my basic objective, the name that I conjured up in my mind as I had stood in the open fields in the starlight close to Maastricht watching the Halifax PM-Q burn. And also thought of each day of the weeks in between then and now. Achievement of that dream was just an arm's length away, surely nothing could stop it now, could it?   Slowly the coach moved through the barrier and on to the road across the open area of the airfield, picking up speed as we progressed; it couldn't have been much more than a mile or so but it seemed to take a lifetime. Then we were there, getting off the coach and standing in the shadow of that huge rock face, on home ground again. Not that it really was home, that had still to come, but it was almost as good as and would do for the time being.

The British border control staff took us inside the adjoining building at once. Questions were to be answered: Who was I and where had I come from?, What was my reason for coming here? and so on. Was I importing any currency? 'Well, yes, a few pesetas.' That was of little consequence. 'Anything else?' 'Mmm. Yes, some French francs.' 'You can't bring those in, we will take them and I will give you a receipt.' I produced the currency, for which I received a sheet of paper headed 'Defence (finance) Regulations'. I was rather peeved about this until I read 'Traveller's Declaration of Money brought into Gibraltar for Subsequent Export', which cheered me up no end for I could get the bank notes back when I left to go home.

The formalities were over. Or were they? Where was Sergeant Alexis Stadnik our Russian companion? He had been with us when we arrived, where was he now? He had disappeared. Before getting back on the coach to continue our journey to the RAF camp we wanted an answer. 'Where is Alexis, he was here with us a minute or two ago?' One of the border control officers said: 'Oh he has gone off in a car up to the Governor's Palace.' We never saw Sergeant Stadnik again.

In total contrast it was back into the coach and a gentle crawl up to RAF quarters. Pilot Officer Lorne Kropf, Sergeant Michael Joseph Joyce and Sergeant Gordon Mellor rejoined the Royal Air Force as we passed through the entrance gates. It was in the afternoon of 26 October 1942. The pilot officer was directed one way and Mike and I another. Quarters were allocated to us, and after settling in Mike and I took the opportunity to investigate the town. We had been given an advance of pay as we had only a few Spanish pesetas between us on arrival. The sight of a policeman on duty in the main street in virtually the same uniform and helmet as in London prompted me to make immediate use of a telegraph office to send home a message that all was well. I did not wish to wait for the official sources to do so.

Next morning, encouraged by the sunshine and the salty breeze, Mike and I wandered through the camp down to the water's edge and to the adjoining slipway where a Catalina flying boat was drawn up out of the sea. I had always been intrigued by its unusual shape and wanted to take a closer look. As we approached the aircraft a familiar figure appeared on board; it turned out to be Dicky Fairly, who had been with us during training in Canada. His passage across the North Atlantic had been marred by continuous bouts of sea sickness and, now, here he was an experienced navigator serving in flying boats in Coastal Command. Having been in the far north flying with the Russian convoys, his crew were now using Gibraltar as a staging post much as Mike and I were. He had difficulty in accepting that my companion and I were in civilian clothes. I had to say something so I used the term 'special duties' and followed it up with a request to look at the working area inside the Catalina. This he agreed to and we climbed aboard to marvel at the spacious accommodation for the navigator and also the excellent observation facilities. I was amused to see a stain from a blob of tomato sauce that had escaped from a sandwich on to the chart. A long plot showed that they had carefully navigated around it where it stood directly in their correct path. We parted with the hope of seeing each other again, but we never have.

It was now time for us to set about getting ourselves kitted out in uniform and acquiring some of the necessities of service life; already having the advance of pay indicated that we still had our priorities in the right order. We had no duties to fulfil for we were only passing through and it was a question of waiting until repatriation was arranged. There was no sign of Alexis Stadnik or of Pilot Officer Kropf.

Saturday, 31 October seemed as if it was to follow the pattern of previous days, but by late morning the news that we were to join a US Army Air Corps Dakota (C47) flight to the UK that night brightened our outlook and the appointed hour to be ready to move off could not come quickly enough. I did use some of the time to return to the Revenue Office to reclaim the French francs that had been taken from me on arrival. There was no difficulty as I was leaving the area. After dark transport arrived promptly to carry Mike and me down to the airfield, picking up Lorne Kropf on the way. I had acquired a kitbag to carry the suit that I had worn continuously since leaving Liège, a number of items that had been issued to me and a few purchases from the town. The other two were similarly lightly stocked. The waiting proved to be intolerable. Eventually a group of perhaps fifteen or sixteen people gradually gathered together on the tarmac in the darkness to board the aircraft. 'Sit where you like' was the only instruction from the NCO supervising the group's entry. There was no particular advantage in this offer for the plane was fitted out for carrying paratroops in two long lines, one on each side of the cabin, leaving a clear central gangway with the passengers sitting sideways facing into the central space. The seats were shaped to take a parachute with the troopers sitting on them. We did not have parachutes. Consequently the passengers slipped to the bottom of the seat unless one had a suitable coat to roll up to fill the void. No? Then you would not find it comfortable. Only with the start up of the two engines did my impatience recede, sufficiently to note that take-off was at thirty-five minutes after midnight. The windows along the fuselage had been blacked out so there was no last glimpse of darkened Gibraltar or the lights of the southern tip of Spain.

Time passed slowly as we climbed to something like 10,000ft and with it came a considerable drop in temperature. The seats were unpleasant, increasingly so, and everybody was cold; except the crew, of course, they were well prepared, having done this trip many times before. The interior lights were not bright enough to read by and boredom set in. One's horizon was limited to the man sitting opposite some 5 or 6ft away. Conversation had not been animated, but now it faltered and died. If only it wasn't so cold. I must have visualised every mile until, through a badly fitting piece of blackout on a porthole, a chink of daylight became visible. Was it getting warmer or was this just imagination?

No information on the route had been available, but it must have taken us through the Strait of Gibraltar out into the Atlantic until we could pass well to the seaward side of Portugal and across open sea to the UK. With luck we would not encounter a German air patrol, yet it could happen. What an ironic twist that would be. Once had been enough and after all the many miles that we had already travelled, coming down in the sea would be the last straw.

It was now getting warmer and the aircraft was gradually losing height. A bank to starboard, several more manoeuvres, then the whine of the undercarriage going down, followed by the rumble of wheels on the runway, and we had made it. But where were we for goodness sake?

It was twenty mintues past eight in the morning, so the flight had been of seven and three quarter hours' duration; if the rumour was correct we were at Portreath in Cornwall. The sergeant in charge of the cabin confirmed the speculation; he also added that this was a stop to visit customs and passport control – we would then re-embark and fly on to Aldermaston, their USAF base. So we descended from the plane and walked across the tarmac towards the cluster of buildings. While doing so our attention was directed towards the runway, just in time to see a twin-engined monoplane streak along it and take off; this was my first sighting of a de Havilland Mosquito. It flew off at a great rate.

For the official entry into our own country, they did not seem too perturbed by the fact that neither Mike nor I had any documents – RAF Gibraltar had not issued us with a 1250 form. Obviously we were not the first to come through with a similar recent history and our few possessions were of no interest. This bleak airfield felt familiar, but there was no joy in it. In a very short time those uncomfortable seats reclaimed us and the pilot, Captain Daniels, wished to get back to his base as soon as he could. Another take-off and another hour and thirty-five minutes in the air and we had made a landing, this time at the American base of Aldermaston in West Berkshire.

As soon as the engines were off and the propellers had finished turning, a variety of vehicles were there for the unloading. One Jeep was waiting for the three of us; after the enquiry as to whether we had eaten or not the driver pulled up outside a large single-storey building. Inside was a vast space filled with dining tables. The room seated in excess of 1,000 people at one sitting and this had already happened, for every table was filled with discarded plates, cups, cutlery and leftovers. It presented a vision of absolute chaos. Certainly not RAF style. We cleared a table and had a very good meal.

It seems that we had lost all the other passengers from the aircraft, whoever they were. The final service that we received from the USAF was a swift ride in the Jeep to Reading railway station. A wave of the hand and our driver was gone, swallowed up in the traffic. We were on our own again. Well not quite, as there was always the railway transport officer (RTO) so we made our way to his office. He caused no difficulties at all, but his eyes had opened a bit when his request to see our identity cards could not be fulfilled and we said where we had come from. However, he arranged tickets for us to London, gave us the time of the train and where to report when we reached the city. While lingering on the platform I noticed a woman passenger, also waiting for the same train because she was wearing a pair of RAF flying boots; I wondered how this was arranged. We would never know for sure.

Finally we were at Paddington and took the escalator to the Bakerloo Line. After a couple of stations further to Marylebone, it was then across the road to the Great Central Hotel, now serving as the London transit camp. We went in. The staff on the information desk either knew that we would report there or they were familiar with the procedure to be adopted. We were told that we would not be required until the morning, which was Monday. I was all attention when we were each asked where are homes were. To my answer of 'Wembley' one man said, 'You can go home, but be back tomorrow at nine o'clock in the morning.' The others were to stay at the transit camp, but I went off, feeling lucky for this freedom. Before I could reach the station for the train to my home town I was stopped by a two-man RAF Service Police (SP) patrol, resulting in the usual request for one's 1250 and leave pass; I had neither. Surely I was not going to be held up on the last few miles of my journey. In the end they must have thought that my story was too outrageous not to be true, or perhaps it was when I offered to take them back to the transit centre for confirmation of the explanation that I had given them.

Well I was thankfully on my way again, but not for long. I had walked maybe 50yd with the first patrol barely out of sight, when round a corner came another two SPs, virtually twins of the first pair. I was not going to repeat all that had just transpired, so when they gave every indication that they were going to stop me I hastily said that I had already seen their two companions less than a minute ago. To my astonishment, they smiled and said 'OK.'

Less than an hour later I was walking along Douglas Avenue, the road leading to my home. Daylight was fading fast and the road was deserted, so nobody saw me as I walked up the garden path to knock on the door. My family did not even know that I was in the country; I assumed that the Air Ministry had notified my mother that I was in Gibraltar and that my own telegram had arrived. Obviously not. So my homecoming was a complete surprise, but a great moment. My whole adventure – from the loss of our aircraft and my subsequent escape; all the help received from various resistance organisations; and a final return home to safety – was almost complete. All that was left now was to journey another 160 miles or so back to RAF Elsham Wolds. It was Sunday afternoon, 1 November 1942, and also my twenty-third birthday.

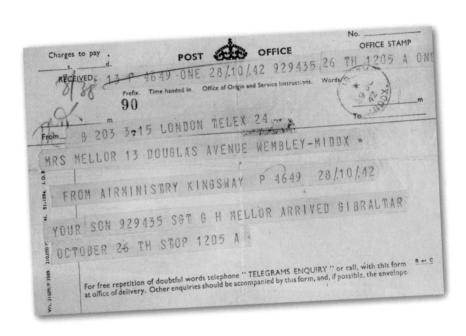

'Arrived Gibraltar.'

Chapter 9

Has Anyone Seen My Greatcoat?

Monday morning came quickly; a night in one's own bed had been a longed-for pleasure, but an early start was necessary to be at the London transit camp in time for the day's events. I joined my two colleagues and entered the room set aside for the expected interview. Two officers in Army uniform appeared; no introductions were made merely, 'Here are paper and pencils – write down your recent experiences.' This could take an hour or two – the day stretched ahead of us – so we got down to it. Yet no more than five minutes elapsed before the instruction came: 'OK stop writing, that will do.' Now what was that all about? Surely they didn't think that our mentalities were so dull that they needed to be sharpened up on the recent past events? They had been uppermost in our thoughts throughout the past weeks. Indeed, would we ever be able to forget them?

I do not recall a get-together in the form of discussion, despite the sharing of experiences as Mike and I had done. One would have sparked the other off and at the same time corroborated the information. The process was more in the style of an individual interview. The period of concern was from after the landing by parachute to our passing into Spain. Notes were taken as each of us gave our version of the progress through the occupied territories; there were no histrionics, just a recitation of facts with dates, names and locations where positively known. Questions regarding any new information to be passed on were included and, with this in mind, I related what I had been told of the deployment of nightfighters to the airfield at Saint-Trond, which drew the quick reaction of 'We already know all about that', which rather brought my interview to a close. Perhaps they had heard it all before –

more than once no doubt – as they were not enthusiastic at all. However, to the residents living within a few minutes' flying time from that base it was of importance and they wanted to be sure the Allies knew about it.

By this time another figure had joined the occupants of the room, in the form of an RAF officer of wing commander rank. His interest was confined to the flying aspects of the operation, none of which had been discussed during the previous interviews. The unusual route to the target was mentioned, as were the signs of the German defence action that I had logged at the time and, in particular, our amazement of the spread of the raid with the need for us to search the area for the aiming point that we were required to attack. Having got this far, the next issues were the tactics of the Me110 nightfighter, our reactions and the result of the whole encounter ending with the order to bale out. I was unable to give any positive information related to the outcome for the other members of the crew. The aircraft had not been very high and was travelling very fast in a descent at the time of baling out and we had not linked up at all once on the ground. Moreover, had anyone else survived?

There was little else that was required of us in this building at this time and we were required to report to the Air Ministry. On arrival we were directed to the correct officer with instructions on where to find him. This we did, and found ourselves seated in a room with a flight lieutenant who was well informed on our situation. First on the agenda was dealing with immediate matters such as identity cards, leave amounting to three weeks, ration cards for that period and travel warrants. This for me was great for I wanted to go back to Elsham to see old friends at the squadron during the period of leave. Finally, we came to the all-important question of what we were to do after the leave period ended. Our futures were about to be sorted out. The flight lieutenant asked each of us what we wanted to do – this was a most unexpected proposition. My reaction was to ask for a pilot's course. He said, 'OK we can fix that.' I also mentioned that my promotion to flight sergeant was months overdue. Another 'OK.' I do not recall what the other two replied but I was well satisfied. As we left, his parting shot was to say that if we had any problems to come back to see him.

Outside on the busy pavement we came to the parting of our ways. Mike had a further interview to attend as he had been a prisoner of war and was then to go on leave to Ireland. We had become quite close over the previous weeks and it would seem strange without his company. There were handshakes all round, for Lorne Kropf was on his way also, and then each one was lost among the many pedestrians in the street.

Leave started from that moment and three weeks stretched out before me like a lifetime, as if it had no end. For a while, as I made my way home, I was saddened that Mike and I had made no promise to meet up again; perhaps he had had his reasons, or maybe he realised that with the vast number of units in the air force that we could be posted to, it was most improbable that we would be reunited by chance, so what was the point.

Living back at home was most enjoyable as always, and on that first evening I took an almost perverse delight in reading through the flood of correspondence and telegrams that had been sent home during my absence, such as from the Air Ministry, RAF Records and the Red Cross. There were also some very kind letters from the squadron CO, Wing Commander R.A.C. Carter, and the Padre, Squadron Leader E.D. Ratledge. Not a pleasant duty for them, for every time a plane failed to return there were seven or eight similar such letters to be written and posted off.

One could not forget the losses that were commonplace in squadron life during the time of conflict. The crews still repeated the frequently heard phrase, 'It will not happen to me', but, unfortunately, all too often it did. Unfeeling as it may seem the gaps left were soon filled with other persons, with new characters and new faces. Those lost were not forgotten, they just were not there any more. Leave time came along, distance travelled away was a separation. A different life to be enjoyed for a few days. Then back to the familiar, which once more had changed.

Many of my friends at home were away serving in one of the three services – Bill Brooker, the Evans boys, also the Holifields and the Holland brothers – however, there was one particular family where I had been welcomed for many years and this was the Clarkes, who lived only a short walk from my home. Kenneth and I were pictured in the same class when we were seven years old and, later, because of the months between our birthdays, not always in the same class but at the same school. Ken was serving in the Sudan at Khartoum and Geoffrey was elsewhere in this country. Their actress sister Daphne, at home at the present time, was often away for many weeks on tour. The show at His Majesty's Theatre in Haymarket, in which she was appearing, was enjoying a London season and, as we had been corresponding for quite a while, an early visit was called for. I must say that I got a very warm reception from both her and her parents.

With the arrival of a letter from the CO asking me to visit the squadron at Elsham, I packed my bag for a short stay and used the travel warrant I had acquired for just that purpose. Off to central London and away to Retford in Nottinghamshire, and then on through the country, passing towns and villages with familiar place names like Gainsborough, Kirton in Lindsey, Brigg and once more to Barnetby. With luck I had a lift up to the airfield and was dropped off next to the sergeants' mess to fix up accommodation for my stay. Many years later I was to read in Don Charlwood's book, *No Moon Tonight*, that my unexpected entry that evening into the mess had become history – for enquiring if anyone had seen my greatcoat, left there the night we went missing. As if anybody would know, of course; there were always dozens of similar coats hanging on the pegs in the entrance hall. Remarkably – after all those weeks absent – I did find it still hanging on a hook, together with a haversack containing my razor, toiletries and other small possessions.

    There were some significant changes at the base, the principal one being the replacement of the Halifax aircraft with Lancasters. Austen Magor, a friend of mine from Lichfield, now a flight lieutenant, had arrived and was the new squadron navigation leader. Similarly, there were two new commanders of 'A' and 'B' flights, both Australian pilots, also from my course at Lichfield: Keith Douglas, later to become CO of 460 Squadron and Colin Rose, to be lost only a couple of months later. The Halifax period, from July to the end of October 1942, had been less than favourable to the squadron, not only because of the fatalities in the crash that I had witnessed, but the failure of our aircraft to return to Elsham had been the eighth incident. During the remainder of October there had been five more crews lost, making thirteen in all – just about 100 men with some crews carrying a second pilot. No wonder there had been few faces that I recognised in the mess that first evening. Of the last raid from 103 Squadron at Elsham, with a Halifax aircraft to Milan, two aircraft had gone down; of these I only knew Squadron Leader Fox's crew, with a particular friend of mine, Warrant Officer Bert Spiller, as their navigator. He was usually known as Dizzy Spiller. Many months later he was also to make a re-appearance in the mess. He was the third navigator from those few weeks on Halifax aircraft at Elsham to evade from the occupied territories of Europe.

Next morning, breakfast time appeared to be the same as it always had been, with that feeling of expectancy in the air of what the day was to bring. There were a few tired faces of men ready for bed, just come off duty or late back after flying the previous night. But they were nearly all strangers; just one or two familiar faces now were dispersed around the dining room. However, WAAF waitresses greeted us cheerfully with a smile – the ever-constant figures there hurrying from table to table at mealtimes, despite the fact that a number of them had lost their boy-friends from this very mess.

I went down through the working camp past the three hangars to the squadron building; inside I had to ease myself through the crush of air-crew gathering there and sought refuge in the adjutant's office. 'Hello, glad you have come, the CO wants to see you. I will tell him you are here.' Within a couple of minutes he was back: 'It's OK you can go in now.' This suited me fine. I knocked on the door and threw up a smart salute. It was a good interview and I was able to answer some of his questions. The flight, the target and the encounter with the nightfighter were easy enough, and also the early days on the ground in Belgium. After that one or two enquiries were on matters that I had been warned to avoid. He seemed to accept that, but was pleased that I had visited for it would help to spread a little confidence that it was possible to make a 'home run'. Seeing the person in the flesh was so much more effective than just hearing about it on the 'grapevine'. Additionally, the station commander wanted to see me.

I had time to renew my acquaintance with the two new flight com-manders, Keith Douglas and Colin Rose, if only for a few minutes each; after all, for them it was a busy working day. That left Austin Magor, the squadron navigation leader – he was in much the same situation as the other two but we managed a little extra time. He raised the question of my family's feelings on my sudden disappearance and those of my girlfriend,

Daphne. With my reply of saying things were going pretty well in that direction and that she worked in the theatre, his face fell into a troubled look; he came back with a very old-fashioned comment: 'Not on the stage?' I had to laugh and eased his mind by saying that I had known her since I was ten years old and that I had been at school with her brother. Some fifty years later he met my wife at a reunion at Elsham and realised his fears had been unfounded.

It was nearly time now to report to the group captain and, as I approached station headquarters, I met one of the officers I had known for many months coming out of the front door. We had a few words, he went his way and I thought to save time I would take a short cut through the main entrance. As soon as my foot touched the front step a loud voice assailed me with: 'Where do you think you are going flight sergeant?' Just when I thought I had managed to avoid him, I was caught by the station warrant officer (SWO), the most influential man on the camp after the CO. 'To see the group captain, sir.' To this his reply was: 'Then you will enter station headquarters by the back entrance as all NCOs and airmen do, is that understood?' 'Yes sir.' 'Then do it or you will be late.' I uttered another 'Yes sir' before ducking round the side of the building to the rear. Luckily I was still on time. He must have known all along where I was heading, little went on that the SWO didn't know about. That little episode must have made his day.

With Group Captain Constantine I could discuss what had happened during the operation and until the time that I had asked the family in Alleur in Belgium if they could give me some assistance. The remainder was in very general terms and I had to avoid places and names until we reached Gibraltar. As with my talk with the squadron CO, he tried to get as much general information as possible without pushing me into a corner; I hoped that he felt satisfied. Other than a few friends he was the first and only one to say 'Good show, a good effort' since I had crossed over from Spain into Gibraltar.

I had previously listed in my mind the people who I wanted to see. The station navigation officer was important to me and, in fact, our meeting proved to be crucial to my future in the RAF. He was greatly pleased to see me enter his office. Early in the conversation he asked me if I had brought back my navigation watch. As I had anticipated that this would be a likely question, I had taken the precaution of leaving it at home and was not wearing it. I expect he, too, had anticipated my reply that it could have been torn off as I baled out through the escape hatch of the Halifax, to which he countered: 'Well we can't give it to you then can we?' I have no doubt that it was written off with all the rest of my gear. The watch was used throughout the remainder of the war and long afterwards and is still a treasured possession.

Now came the question, 'What are you going to do now?', and my answer, 'At the moment I am down for a pilot's course.' The discussion that followed was in the form of several questions, the main two being on the lines of 'Are you satisfied with your present situation and rank?' and 'Are you ambitious to make progress?' The latter held some resonance, for there was only one more rank for me to achieve as an NCO, that of warrant officer. A suggestion was now put forward that I should abandon the idea of becoming a pilot and extend my expertise in navigation by applying for a staff navigators' (SN) course at the Central Navigation School at RAF Cranage. I grasped the idea with both hands and mentally kicked myself for not thinking this through when asked what I wanted to do while at the Air Ministry. I would now have to persuade the flight lieutenant who had raised the original question that this was a much better proposition. Having expressed my thanks for the advice, I left the station navigation office to continue my search for people I owed a visit.

The parachute section was next for me, to be able to assure the packers – who seemed to be mostly WAAFs – that I appreciated their skill and work was 100 per cent, and that my parachute had worked perfectly. When you were falling out of the sky your only hope of survival was the package of silk and cords attached to your body harness. It had to be a success, there was no second chance.

I was nearly done. My penultimate visit was to the operations room to say hello to those on duty, and also to make my apologies to one of the WAAFs who I had arranged to take to a local dance early in October, only for the date to be frustrated by our fateful raid to Aachen. If she had been on duty that night the reason would have been known by daybreak, with our crew being the one name listed on the situation board with no time of landing. However, being off duty this day she was not there, so I left her a message of regret. No doubt, in being very attractive there would have been other invitations over the weeks. It was a state of affairs that became commonplace on front-line squadrons.

My final call took me to the Link Trainer, to have a word with the flight sergeant who supervised the flying training there. He had given up quite a few of his off-duty hours in the evenings for me to become proficient in handling the controls of an aircraft. This, together with some actual dual practice on both Wellington and Halifax aircraft in the air on suitable occasions, was part of our crew's attempt to ensure that each member could take over another crew position in an emergency or injury from enemy fire. At the same time, Robert Hawthorn in the front turret was getting to grips with basic navigation.

Well that was that; I had now made contact with all those I had planned to see. I booked out of the sergeants' mess and set off to leave camp on foot, along the road by the long wood and out of the main gate. No transport was going my way and my bicycle had been taken over by the team who looked after missing airmen's personal effects. In fact, the sergeant in charge had sought me out the previous evening to ask if I had found everything done to be to my satisfaction? It was indeed.

I walked down to Barnetby, as I had done a number of times previously. Even in November it was a fine afternoon. While waiting on the platform for the train I heard – as I had on my first arrival back in May – the sound of Merlin aero-engines warming up beyond the brow of Elsham hill. Ops on tonight? Most likely.

The train arrived, and as it moved on its journey I thought, 'That is that, I am no part of the life there any more. That chapter is closed.' And yet, has that really been so? For even after all these years I still find myself attached to the place and return there with many others in like mood in August each year.

Gordon and Daphne's wedding.

Chapter 10

'Taking Advantage of the Situation'

After my trip to Elsham, being back at home that same evening felt great even in the blackout. But the next morning was a new day, with things to do and new thoughts to turn into fact if at all possible. Now was the time to try and alter the path I would follow in the future. First of all was to attempt to gain entry to the flight lieutenant at the Air Ministry. On arrival in Kingsway this proved to be quite easy. In fact, the man on duty at the front entrance proved most helpful and within a few minutes I was sitting in the office explaining the reasons for my desire to abort the request for a pilot's training course and instead to continue with an SN course at the Central Navigation School, to upgrade my standing and qualification as a navigator. In the background, still being very ambitious, was the desire to move up out of the NCO ranks, but this remained unsaid. For years afterwards I wondered if I should also have expressed this thought there and then. My request for the change received the comment that the new plan would be preferable for the air force and that he could arrange it. The only snag was that there was a waiting list and that I would have to take a temporary posting elsewhere. This was OK by me, for having my preference accepted I was willing to agree to any conditions he might impose. I departed well satisfied and to await the posting, which would come before my leave ended.

There were a further few days of leave remaining, perhaps as many as six or seven, and while at Elsham I had arranged with Flight Sergeant Arthur Tilley that we should meet in London when he also came down on leave. He was a pilot on the squadron and had already been there when I and my crew arrived. He sported a unique flash on the top of the sleeve of his uniform announcing that he was from the Anglo-Egyptian

Sudan. One other pilot followed suit by identifying his origin as Argentina; the latter's jacket was much in demand, presumably to attract attention from the many young ladies on the camp and in the local neighbourhood.

I had already met Arthur and knew that he was at Elsham before being posted there myself, because he was engaged to Mary Budd, a colleague and friend of Daphne Clarke; both girls had Jack Hilton as their agent, and being together in the same shows made our meeting inevitable. I became known to the stage doormen at one or two theatres in London over the next seven months, particularly at His Majesty's in the Haymarket and the Palace along Shaftesbury Avenue. I will always be grateful to performer Eddie Gray's partner, Jack Hartman, for inviting me to invade his dressing room in the theatre during the evening performances when I was home on leave to see Daphne. Also, the Universal Brasserie downstairs below the Criterion Theatre on the south side of Piccadilly Circus was conveniently placed for us, not only for the food but as a meeting place for the many young servicemen and women while on leave in London.

The letter with my posting arrived as promised; where was my destination? I was eager to find out. I ripped the envelope open; it was not back to Elsham then. Instead it was to RAF Staverton, sited between Gloucester and Cheltenham. This raised visions of travelling on the famous Cheltenham flyer on the Great Western line, but in reality journey was less fine by a dilatory train to Gloucester. After a bus ride I arrived outside the main entrance to the camp with all my gear and nobody in sight, but the air was filled with the sound of a Spitfire steeply climbing off the runway. I just had to watch it and thought that it looked as if it had contrarotating propellers. I said aloud 'That's new.' By now the plane was a dot in the sky, so no chance for a second look. Directly behind me there was a large factory building of the Rotol Company. The penny dropped, of course they made propellers; perhaps I had not been mistaken after all. This would not concern my duties, however, but Staverton was no quiet backwater and it looked as if my stay here was going to be most interesting.

The procedure for joining a new RAF station was very much the same wherever it was and so it proved. I was now part of No. 6 Air Observer

School (AOS). The first morning had barely begun before I was being briefed on my new role and was meeting another arrival, Flight Sergeant John Deardon, and also Flying Officer Dickson, under whose wing we were to work. We had a large room with an attached office in a building that gave us a direct view on to the airfield and the main runway. The principal idea was to set up a pre-flight briefing room and procedures based on those in use on RAF stations occupied by operational squadrons, so that the navigators under training became familiar with conditions and procedures that would be commonplace later on. Much was to be done and information to be gathered.

Naturally enough my new companions, especially those I worked with, wanted a quick rundown of my experience in the RAF and to know what I had been doing before being posted to Staverton. I tried to be as discreet as possible, having already been warned by MI9 not to say anything, but a general outline of 'Had to bale out and got back home' proved to be less than satisfactory and only led to further enquiries. Despite my lack of enthusiasm to widen the topic, word got around and shortly afterwards there was a phone message for me to report to the group captain. What had I done now? The only thing was to go and find out. So it was into station headquarters and an OK with the adjutant, before I knocked on the door. 'Come in.' I saluted. 'Flight Sergeant Mellor, sir.' The questions came. Where had I come down, it seemed a general matter of interest. 'Belgium sir', then he asked exactly where. I had been told by Military Intelligence not to discuss these details with anyone. What could I do except communicate that? It was not a good move. Perhaps I should have softened my reply a bit. I felt that he considered it an affront to himself, because shortly after he drew the interview to a close. Perhaps I had given him little opportunity to do otherwise.

One or two people appreciated my reluctance to give details, but the rest had little idea of security, and a morsel of information was good for the conversation and ego over a drink in a public bar among friends and could be heard by anyone else. It was only a few short weeks since I had been walking the streets of Brussels and Paris and other occupied towns, travelling on trams and trains within touching distance of the German military and whomever they employed. Could information be in danger of being passed back to mainland Europe? I supposed it was possible. So I did not wish to increase the risk of penalties facing our helpers in the occupied nations. Notices such as that translated below, were prominently displayed in those countries:

AVIS [Notice]
Any male persons directly or indirectly helping the crews of enemy aircraft landed by parachute or having effected a forced landing, or assisting in the evasion, or hiding or helping them, in any way whatever, will be shot immediately.

Women guilty of the same offence will be deported to concentration camps in Germany.

Any person seizing crew members having effected a forced landing or descending by parachute, or who, by their attitude, contributes to their capture, will receive a reward up to 10,000 francs. In some special cases this reward will be even higher.

Paris, 22 September 1941.

The Military Governor in France
Signed: von Stulpnagel
Infantry General.

John and I found that we were gradually left to run the briefing room and its activities on our own, including planning the routes suitable for the airborne exercises required by the instructors. The many pilots available came from different backgrounds: Polish, Czech, British and even American. Some of the central European pilots had acquired several thousand hours' flying time each in peacetime; one could not help being envious of their vast experience. This airfield was a very active environment, for not only was there Rotol using a variety of aircraft in their research work on propellers, but across the airfield there was yet another organisation, led by Sir Alan Cobham, developing in-flight refuelling.

Some 2 miles or so away to the south of Staverton, beyond the local high point of Churchdown Hill, was sited another airfield known as

Brockworth, protected by a balloon barrage, where jet aircraft were being developed. It was necessary to warn those operating the balloons of departure and return times whenever Staverton Ansons were flying exercises, to ensure the balloons were close-hauled for the safety of our crews. Little information of the activities at Brockworth leaked out. We had met two of the test pilots many times at Peter's Bar in Cheltenham for a few games of darts. But there was no loose talk by them, and they were sharp players with a very good eye.

In the new year information gradually became available regarding the rest of my crew. While I was still missing, my family had been in touch with the British Red Cross Society, but it was too early to expect a positive reply. However, once it became known that I was in Gibraltar, speculation spread among the next of kin of the other crewmembers that we must have come down in the Mediterranean. Other than saying this was not so I had no news of their fate at all. When I was staying in Liège with Jeannie and Mathilde I heard that three airmen prisoners of war had passed through the town and that one of them had a brown complexion. Were they members of my crew? The description of the man with the brown skin sounded like our skipper, Warrant Officer Edwards. I couldn't say so then or later when back home.

Towards the end of January 1943 I received a letter saying that Flight Sergeant Robert Hawthorn was a POW and giving me the address of Stalag Luft VIIIB. Nothing about the others. So I wrote off to him the most guarded and innocent of letters; within a week it was back with me, returned by the censor. How could that be? I was stumped. Perhaps it was only because I put the letter into the post box on the camp at Staverton. Some months later I received a letter directed to my home address from the British Red Cross. It gave me the information that at last they had received the news from Geneva of the burial place of Eddie Edwards, our pilot, and George Green, the flight engineer, as being situated in the cemetery at Saint-Trond in Belgium. That was now three of them accounted for. And so it remained for more than two years.

Relationships back in Wembley took a more serious turn when Daphne and I decided to tell the two families that we intended to get married. I skipped the tradition of asking her father for permission; I don't think he noticed – he was delighted, as was the rest of the near family. Arrangements for the wedding had to be made, and I was thankful to be at a safe distance in Gloucestershire, but I was available to go to the registrar in Harrow to get the marriage licence. I remember the cost was seven shillings and six pence. Unfortunately I had only one-pound notes and the registrar had given up all her small change to previous callers. So Daphne had to pay out the required sum. From that day it has always remained a debt. I hope that she's always felt that she got a bargain.

As the spring progressed I was called upon to fly as an instructor, and a few times as the staff navigator, ferrying various RAF officers to and from other stations within range of the Ansons. On one occasion we were returning to Staverton with a group captain on board. Fog was forming quickly on the ground and we were flying directly towards the sun, which was very low. The visibility was deteriorating, so while I relied on my calculated route to fly, I was supplementing it with a sharp lookout for recognisable features on the ground – for as soon as the airfield came in sight we would need to approach and land with the minimum delay. We were on course so there was little more to do. I filled in the time with map reading as a safety measure; this seemed to concern our passenger enough to ask if I had yet finished my training. That was a knock to one's self-esteem. However, having said 'Yes indeed,' I asked him if he had noticed the fog gathering below. Sitting in the middle of the fuselage he probably had not. With the Anson descending as we passed over Cheltenham, to land shortly afterwards, I hoped he felt happier. I was satisfied with the result. Being back on time meant that I could attend the entertainment that evening at nearby Innsworth WAAF camp. It was a very foggy walk back to Staverton camp that night.

One of the sergeant pilots from the USA, who had arranged to be transferred out of the RAF into the air force of his own country and was now an officer, returned for a short visit and set me thinking that he had made a good career move. There were still a few months to pass before I would be promoted to warrant officer rank, and that there was no further promotion except in a commissioned capacity. With no sign of a Second Front invasion of France for a year or two at least, I needed to think seriously about my future. Peacetime, attractive as the thought was, could still be years away. Now was the time to try and shape my future, although my prospects may be better after taking the SN course at the Central Navigation School. I decided that I should make an approach to become a commissioned officer at this time.

The route to be followed seemed rather strange. I was told that I had to write a note to my present CO asking for permission to fill in an application form. If he approved I could then fill in that appropriate form and so start the sequence of interviews with successively senior officers, starting with the chief instructor, through the group captain, to the group commander, probably an air commodore. The first step was taken and prompted a telephone call to report to my immediate senior straight away; this I did. He was in a general office with a number of other ranks present there. As he was newly arrived at Staverton this was to be my first time of seeing him – except that it wasn't. I knew him immediately for he was an RCAF flying officer and had been the course instructor of one-half of our detachment to Navigation School at Port Albert in Ontario. With others within listening range, and after a couple of questions about my experiences, he said: 'I am not putting this forward; you do not get a commission for good service or good work.' I had thought that these qualities would be a good basis to start with. He didn't enlighten me as to what he thought were adequate grounds, and knowing his attitude to other ranks I was not surprised he wouldn't change his mind. So that was that. I was disappointed at not being able to progress any further but, being summarily dismissed, realised that I would not be there very much longer and there would surely be another opportunity. Later, as an afterthought, I considered that he was well out of order; to my mind the interview should have been held in private and not within the hearing of others, some of whom were junior to me in rank. However, I was sure there would be another time and another place. Before leaving the room, to ensure that he knew me I did ask him if he had any news of Flying Officer Coupland, who had been the instructor for my half of the contingent for training in Canada. His reply was, 'Oh yes you were at Port Albert of course. He is somewhere in Iceland flying Hudsons or something similar.' And so ended that episode.

I spent much time searching Cheltenham for suitable accommodation for living off camp after Daphne and I were married. I was not having much luck there as yet, nor in Gloucester. Yet there was some relief, for Daphne was in a new show that had been in rehearsal and was having a two-week run at a theatre in Oxford before opening at the Palace Theatre in London. On two weekends I was able get leave after duty on Friday and go to Oxford to see Daphne and stay at the same theatrical digs, where they still had accommodation unoccupied. On both occasions I cycled the distance through villages such as Northleach, Windrush and Burford, which was most enjoyable except on the last return journey on a Sunday afternoon. I was facing into a strong westerly wind all the way back that prevented me from coasting down the hills, so it was a matter of pedalling the whole way; 40-plus miles was no joke. I even tried to thumb a lift off an occasional overtaking lorry, but the bicycle must have put them off, for there were no offers.

Time was passing and the agreed wedding date was getting ever closer. Then my luck changed, for one of the WAAF clerks, whose home was by chance in the local area, said that before she joined up she and her sister had shared a flat at the top of a house in the centre of Cheltenham. Perhaps it was available. Having obtained the address from her, I was on my bike at the first opportunity. I found Osmond Terrace, which ran parallel to the fashionable road known as the Promenade. And the number? Ah, Yes, there it was. The front garden looked pretty grotty, but now that I was here I should see what the house was like. The front door opened and my introduction and enquiries resulted in being asked into the house.

Many years ago, in the time of horses and carriages, it had been a grand house with four floors and requiring many domestic staff. Now it appeared to be occupied by this single lady and a vast quantity of antiques and collectables filling every horizontal surface within sight. It was obvious that she was a dealer and hoped to sell on the results of her buying expeditions. I did not show much enthusiasm, especially when she said that we would go and look at the flat above. Every step of the staircase was narrowed at each end by a mini collection of her stock-in-trade, leaving just enough space for two feet to pass up. My difficulty in climbing the stairs prompted her to agree to clear the stairs entirely. This sounded promising and so was the flat on the top floor, being surprisingly clean, neat and tidy. On return to the ground floor we discussed rent terms and, having stressed the need to clear the hall and stairs of her goods, I left to telephone Daphne to see if she could come down to Gloucester at the weekend.

There were only ten or twelve days before the wedding so we agreed to take the flat, paid an advance on the rent and left feeling happy that a major obstacle had been overcome. Oh yes, the hall and stairs were clear. It was a remarkable transformation for which I complemented the owner, but I did not enquire as to where everything had gone.

Two days before the wedding, eight of my colleagues – both officers and senior NCOs – gathered in the Osmond Restaurant with me for an evening meal to celebrate the coming nuptials and, considering that we were in the middle of a world war, the catering was extremely good and a 'jolly' time was had by all. On Tuesday, 6 July 1943, my extended leave commenced and I was off to Wembley for the next day's event. Don Jennings, the Australian pilot from Tasmania who was injured on our crash at Lichfield way back in February 1942, arrived from Morpeth in North Yorkshire at my home in Wembley more or less at the same time as myself. Daphne's parents, who lived nearby, had arranged a pre-wedding party, so after a quick smarten up we escorted my mother to the celebrations.

On Wednesday 7 July 1943, Daphne and I were married in the morning at Park Lane Methodist church by the Revd Arthur Cornwall, a friend of Daphne's family, who had travelled down from Derbyshire to take the service. My brother Joseph willingly took up the task of best man. By evening time the reception, the speeches, the good wishes and the farewells were said and Daphne and I were already settled into the Lion Hotel in Shrewsbury. And while there was always one person in a family who liked to sabotage a newly-wed couple's bags with handfuls of confetti, on this occasion he was outsmarted.

A further railway journey took us across Wales to Barmouth, followed by a local train up the coastal line towards Harlech. The nearest railway station to our destination was Dyffryn Ardudwy, where we left the train. There was a porter in charge who explained that there was no taxi available. So, where was Mrs Jones at Gorsdolgau? A smile broke out over his face as he took me to the edge of the platform and, pointing up the line, he said: 'You see that bridge up there?' 'Yes.' 'I can tell you that Gorsdolgau is on the right-hand side beyond that bridge. You will be all right; there are no more trains for two or three hours.' The bridge was tiny in the distance, but there was no alternative. We took hold of our bags and set off along the sleepers of the single track towards the bridge. A little further on, where the line crossed a farm road, was the farm, some 200yd away.

Our new marriage had one more surprise for us. Having made ourselves known to Mrs Jones, she said that a telegram had come for me. It was brief and to the point: 'Course commences 24th July.' At least I was not being recalled directly, spoiling our honeymoon. I later learned that one of my colleagues back at Staverton had put in some powerful appeals on my behalf to revise an order for immediate return. I was most grateful.

The Welsh vacation drew to a close. It had been sprinkled with hill walks and some less energetic days on the superb, lonely beach with only the sound above the country quiet of the occasional aircraft on approach to landing at RAF Llanbedr just up the coast. Two days early we got off the train at Cheltenham and took up residence at the flat. It was only going to be for one or two nights, and as soon as I had closed my connection with Staverton we would be off again. That's how it was; with my travel warrant and posting instructions to RAF Cranage in hand, it was the next step into the future.

Luck was again with us, for Daphne's parents had relations living no more than 2 miles from the airfield and while we had been away had arranged for us to stay with one of these families. So we were off to Birmingham, Crewe and then to Holmes Chapel in Cheshire. The following morning, the 24th, I was on my bike and reporting into the Central Navigation School, on time as required. Preliminaries were completed, a living-out pass arranged, and, most importantly, contact made with the other course members, some sixteen in total and a mixed bag of senior NCOs and commissioned officers. First impressions could be misleading, but with these men there was a keen competitive air to each one and a need to get the most out of the course.

Next morning at 08.00 hours we started the first day of the next twelve weeks. A quick look round to see where everybody had chosen to sit left me thinking that none of us were alike; what on earth did we have in common other than all being navigators? Sure, there was that competitive air noticed yesterday, but for the rest we would have to wait and see as the days and weeks passed. All the basic skills acquired previously were now taken to a higher level; new problems were resolved and a wider range of allied subjects approached, particularly in astro-navigation and time, radio and radar aids, coastal tides, and meteorology and forecasting. Would we complete everything in time?

With the warm summer weather and clear skies in the evenings, it was pleasant to go out into the meadow opposite the house where we were staying with a sextant and star charts, there to view and take sights and readings on a variety of stars and planets – homework of course. On more than one occasion we found that cows had been turned out into the far side of this particular field after evening milking and were unseen by us in the darkness. The intermittent flashing of my torch and our voices acted as a magnet, and the sheer curiosity of the cattle would result in us being entirely surrounded by the herd in a ring, all facing inwards towards Daphne and myself, and munching as if we were to be the next items on their menu.

Of course it was not all lectures and desk work for we were back flying frequently on Ansons. These were probably the most-used aircraft in the air force, superb for all-round visibility and reliability, and ideal for putting into practice what had been the subject of previous lectures. In a lighter mood for summer evenings, there was in Holmes Chapel a hotel with a good restaurant and bar called the Good Companions, based of course on J.B. Priestley's novel of the same name. Alternatively, the city of Manchester was some 18 to 20 miles to the north for a very occasional Saturday visit, with perhaps a matinee at one of the theatres.

In the second half of the course a new discipline made its appearance, in the form of lecture techniques and presentation. Previous acquaintance with these had been as a receiver of information given by others and, while the quality of delivery had varied, where it had not been quite as good as one could have wished, any deficiencies could be made good by additional personal reading of manuals or discussion with other trainees. Now this was the reverse situation and expectations on this course were high. Any inhibitions of standing in front of a group had to be overcome. So we each had several opportunities to prepare and deliver lectures on set subjects. Despite being used to briefing trainee navigators before flying an exercise, I found that by the end of the course my progress in presentation could have been greater; neither the instructor nor I were completely satisfied with my introductory remarks – they needed to be more innovative – but that would come with more experience. At least that was my hope and intention, and fortunately I was delighted with my results achieved from the rest of the course.

After an evening of celebration with the course members and a number of the instruction staff at the local pub in Lower Peover, the next day was a final bicycle ride into camp to gather up my flying kit, navigation gear and books. Then once leave passes and travel warrants for the journey back to Wembley had been collected, it was time to take the final leave of my companions. As always we parted with expressions of hope to meet again, but we never did. All in all, though, it had been an excellent three months.

Sixty-eight years after the event Gordon approaches the door of M. and Mme Van Meeuwen.

Chapter 11

To School on Sunday

Despite the fact that leave had been granted for only seven days, our next placement was to be received during that time. My next posting was to No. 1 Observer Advanced Flying Unit (OAFU) based at RAF Wigtown in Galloway, Scotland. At least it wasn't Northern Ireland, but it was pretty close. Included with the destination were a few more days' leave, which was gratefully received for it gave us more time to make arrangements. Daphne was travelling up with me so a room was booked at the Crown Royal Hotel in Newton Stewart, a town on the railway line to Stranraer. Being October it was quite dark when we reached the station and descended from the train; there was little light in the booking office and, save a bleary, spluttering, faint gas lamp well concealed from the sky on the platform, the blackout was complete. Following directions given by the booking clerk the two of us, laden with bags, gas masks and my bicycle, stepped out into this dark void. Leaving the station approach we turned left downhill towards the main road where a faint glimmer of light indicated that our journey's end was not far now.

Perhaps we should have been warned by the dimness of the sole electric light in the entrance lobby, for not only was the light very poor but the service at the desk was not any better. After several rings on the bell we were at last attended by an austere lady who performed the necessary registration requirements and directed us to our room after saying that we could have a meal in the dining room in half an hour. With that she disappeared through a door and the building returned to silence, except for my muttered remarks on carrying the bags up the staircase. Daphne and I found the dining room because it had the only other light that appeared to be on. There were no other diners to greet as we sat down in the now familiar gloom and awaited the meal. We were hungry, having been travelling all day, and did not wait in vain for the main dish arrived quite quickly. We sat in solitary splendour in the chilly, dim room. I felt no urge to go out and get our bearings with the remainder of the town; that could wait for daylight hours.

During breakfast the following morning I sorted out the best route to cycle to RAF Wigtown, which appeared to be some 8 miles away. Leaving Daphne at the hotel, with Newton Stewart to explore, I set off down the main road running almost due south. It was a fine morning for me to make my acquaintance with the countryside. My route had undulating fields to my right and, opposite, a large flat area where the river mouth had silted up. The River Cree twisted its way down to Wigtown Bay and the open Irish Sea, while the whole was dominated by a massive hump known locally as Cairnsmore of Fleet. I saw Wigtown ahead of me on top of a hill, which on this occasion I was able to avoid by taking a lane that ran to the side at a lower level. I coasted down past a single house named Fordbank, standing in its own grounds, then on to the village of Bladnoch. The large building to my right was a distillery. Facing me was the bridge over the River Bladnoch, which I was to become quite familiar with, but, beyond, the road rose sharply up the side of the valley; this defeated me and I had to dismount from my bicycle and push it to the top. In later weeks, when necessary, I was able to ride up, but by that time I had fitted my machine with a choice of gears.

Within a few minutes more I was sweeping into the camp entrance and reporting into the guard room. Formalities were completed quite quickly and I received instructions on how to reach the staff who needed to know of my arrival. All the buildings close by in the adjoining area were of the domestic camp and I needed to pass on to the working area around the station headquarters. So it was off downhill along the shadowy tree-lined entrance road before shooting out on to the vast open space of the airfield. There was the flying control tower and the bulk of the hangars, and further away was a jumble of low buildings where I would find the people that I had to contact. The lane closely followed the line of the perimeter track and then I was there, ready to join the staff. It was done rapidly, including a living-out pass, which saved them finding me accommodation in a camp that was already short of living space. After a visit to the chief navigation instructor, and a pleasant introduction, it was on to the instruction centre where I was to attach myself to a Flying Officer Waern. He was already expecting me.

After a formal entry to his office, I was greeted by him and introduced to Warrant Officer Peter Wright. The day still had time to give me some surprises. The two men were interested to know what sort of person was joining them for long periods of the day, every day; we were going to have to be in tune with each other. It was up to me to give them a summary of my experience and background. They were both mature, friendly men and listened to my potted history with attention that heartened me greatly. I felt that I had pitched my introduction to my new partners more or less at the right level and in return I received an equally informative response. First, Flying Officer Waern revealed that he too had served on 103 Squadron, but before it moved to Elsham Wolds. He was a career aviator in the RAF, already flying on Fairey Battles with the squadron previous to the outbreak of war on 3 September 1939. As 103 had been one of the bomber squadrons sent to France as part of the British Expeditionary Force (BEF) air component early in September, he had been on operational service from the very beginning until being ordered back to England at the critical Dunkirk period in time. Flying on operations on Wellingtons from RAF Newton in succeeding months, he and his crew had ditched in the North Sea and spent three cold, wet and very uncomfortable days and nights in a dinghy before being rescued. On top of that he wore the ribbon of the Distinguished Flying Medal, which said everything as far as I was concerned. Warrant Officer Peter Wright was brief, but the second surprise of this morning's introduction came from him in that he too had evaded and escaped from enemy-occupied Europe with the help of Andrée de Jongh, as I had less than three months later. Tenuous as the connections were, a lasting relationship was established there and then.

The rest of that first day was used in gleaning much-needed local knowledge of the camp, the training and flying structure in general and plentiful advice on the accommodation situation in the local villages. From the education centre, the county town of Wigtown was clearly visible, occupying the hilltop not much more than 2 miles away. I decided that this was the place to commence our search for rooms or whatever was available to provide us with a home. So breaking the journey back to

Newton Stewart, I cycled up the hill where I discovered that Wigtown was a very compact place, packed around a central square on the only level area there. It also contained two hotels: the Commercial Hotel and the Galloway Arms. I made my approach to the first named and met Mr Macrae, the landlord. Yes, they could take us for the period that it took us to arrange more permanent lodgings. It was arranged that we would arrive the next evening. So it was back to Newton Stewart for one more night. Daphne had found that the town was very full with military and RAF families and so suitable accommodation was scarce. Fortunately we now had other plans.

After the next day's work had finished, Daphne and I transferred with our baggage to the Commercial Hotel in the centre of Wigtown. Certainly the shorter route into the camp in the morning was welcomed, especially after being given a quiet word in the mess that there was an alternative entrance on to the airfield. Having crossed the bridge over the river by the Bladnoch distillery, one could turn left on to a farm road along the riverbank, to find that where it ran on to the airfield, the barbed-wire coils sealing off the boundary had been rearranged enough for a bicycle to pass through. Not all personnel living out had a car, so for those of all ranks in this situation who relied on two wheels it was a popular diversion and avoided the steep hill on the major road passing the main entrance.

While I was on duty at the airfield Daphne searched the town and the outlying properties for the accommodation that we required. The local people were friendly and, following up some advice, she eventually found what we were looking for at a house on a lane, perhaps a mile or so away from the centre of town. It was known as Fordbank House, the same place that I had noticed on my way to the camp on my first morning in the neighbourhood. We would be able to move in to rooms there some days later.

Meanwhile, Mrs Macrae, wife of the hotel owner, presided over the dining room at the time of high tea, which was more substantial than afternoon tea and replaced a later evening meal. On one such evening, when conversation with other guests had temporarily died away, I took the opportunity to ask her if she could tell me how long it would take to visit a small village named Ravenstone. In a flash she asked me who I knew there for it consisted of only one or two properties. In reply I said that the lady's name was Mrs Hawthorn. I had yet to make contact and meet her, but I understood that she was the teacher at the local school. To my amazement the exchange immediately became most direct and the air highly charged.

Her next comment was: 'Her son is in the air force, did you know?'

'Yes I did know that.'

'He is now a prisoner of war in Germany.'

'Yes, we have written to each other.'

With eyes set to pierce me like arrows, she exclaimed: 'Oh! You know him then?'

'Yes we were in the same squadron and in the same crew.'

'He has been in chains for three months.'

Careful now, sparks were beginning to fly. 'I know this has been happening but I was not aware that he personally was involved. That's tough.'

'You weren't there with him when the plane was shot down then?'

'Yes, I was, but I haven't seen him since we baled out.'

'Why not?'

'We probably landed miles apart. The plane swept on, then swung round and crashed a mile or so away from me; there was nothing I could do there so I walked out of the area across country all night, and continued the next night and so on.'

'And after that?'

'Ah, that's confidential and secret, and I can't talk about it but, much later, I did get a lift from Gibraltar with the American air force back home to England.'

My last comment seemed to reduce the tension and to my relief brought an end to the conversation, which had been sparked off by what I thought was an innocent question. I didn't know of the connection between the Macraes and Mrs Hawthorn, but I could now guess that they were close friends. The answer to my query as how to get there and how long it would take went unanswered.

Two days later Mrs Macrae attracted my attention and asked if I was on duty on Sunday, to which I replied that I wasn't. To my delight she told me that she and her husband would take Daphne and I to Ravenstone to see Mrs Hawthorn on that afternoon and that it was all arranged. I told her that we would be most pleased to accept, for this was a most

generous invitation. As indeed it was, for they had a full-time job running the hotel and also only a small ration of petrol for private motoring, as fuel was in very short supply at that time.

And so, on Sunday afternoon Daphne and I set off with Mr and Mrs
Macrae in their motor car from Wigtown, taking a route down through
Bladnoch on the familiar road past the main entrance to RAF, now known
to me by its local name, Baldoon. The road from this point was unfa-
miliar, but after passing through Sorbie some 6 or 7 miles further on we
turned off on to a road signposted for Ravenstone. It was only a few minutes' drive now between hedgerows and past farms and small woods
before a lonely building adjoining a crossroads appeared, sitting in the
open countryside. Coming to a gentle halt I could see that it was the local
schoolroom with the house attached, and there was a warm welcome from
its occupant.

It must have been very difficult for Mrs Hawthorn to retain her com-
posure, with her son a POW in Germany and me sitting down opposite
her at the tea table. During the ensuing talk it was revealed that some of
the next of kin of the crewmembers had been in contact with each
other, exchanging any available scrap of information – not that there
had been much at any time. I understand that as soon as I stepped foot
on Allied territory at Gibraltar a message had been passed back to the
UK, and then on to the families. The mention of Gibraltar had led to
false expectations that we had been on a mission to the Mediterranean
and had come down in the sea. With the vagaries of the postal and telegraph services my mother seemed to be the last to be officially informed.
In fact, my own telegram from the Rock to say where I was, arrived home
before any official notification.

The posting into the area where 'Twiggy' Hawthorn's home was situated happened by chance as far as I was concerned, but having visited his
mother and been welcomed by her, Daphne and I resolved that we would
maintain a close contact with her so that she would feel that she had a
personal relationship with the RAF, rather than the isolated situation of
being 'next of kin'. Over the following months the friendly association
born on that first visit developed and we spent several weekends in her
company, even to now and then taking part in local events held in the
adjoining schoolroom on a Saturday evening. By changing into civilian

clothes it became easier to integrate with the local farmers and their wives, for whom the evenings were really organised.

Not long after I joined the instructional staff, my promotion to warrant officer was promulgated, some two months after its effective date. At this time of the war the rank was highly desired, there being only a very few on each RAF station. The pay was of course better than previously, and there were other small advantages in the mess. The badge of rank was now the royal coat of arms, and the distinctive uniform had to be measured for and tailored. However, one little development regarding uniforms tickled my feelings. After my new uniform was ordered, time flowed on until I was having to ask the flight sergeant in the stores building how much longer it was likely to be before it was delivered. The answer was that it always took time. Yet the same flight sergeant was also promoted during my waiting period and, low and behold, just a week later he was sporting a new WO's uniform. The excuse was that it was a reject sent because it fitted him near enough – but rather well I considered. Having had my suspicions I let it lie, as there was no point in falling out with him over it and my wait for a uniform continued.

By then we were well settled in at Mr and Mrs MacMaster's rooms at Fordbank House and had use of all the facilities of a large kitchen with the housekeeper's welcome agreement. It was a shorter journey into camp in the mornings, and in the evenings it eliminated the need to push the bicycle up the steep hill into Wigtown. With the grounds falling away from the house we had a fine view from our front sitting room and, fortunately, we avoided being under the direct flight path of the low-flying Ansons approaching to land. We were very lucky in finding such a place to live.

With little warning adjustments became necessary in the navigation instruction pattern, brought about to ease the constant demand on aircraft for exercises, both during each morning and afternoon, as well as at night-time for those who were sufficiently advanced. The changes certainly affected us, for one morning Flying Officer Waern came back from a meeting with the chief instructor to say that we had a new job and were moving out from the lecture block into another building, which housed the remains of a DR Trainer. The task was to transform it into an active exercise unit to give simulated air navigation experience, reflecting as close as possible actual flying requirements and problems without leaving the ground. That was what was wanted, so we needed to go and look at the inside of the building and get a good measure of the problems to be resolved.

Waern already had the keys, and despite the lack of use the lock turned easily and we were inside the entrance lobby. With the power on the simple layout was quickly revealed. To the right a single door opened into a large square room with a platform along two adjoining walls, and in the corner of these walls stood a control room. Along the platform stood five double cubicles in both directions, each double unit providing working space for two trainees facing each other, but with one at floor level and the other lifted on to the platform. So the normal course size of twenty men could be completely accommodated in the one room. The other doorway in the opposite wall of the lobby revealed another room of similar size and layout. We would be able to take forty trainees maximum in two separate exercises on any morning or afternoon; if we had the staff of course. There was little residue from previous users; a few navigation charts, two or three with samples of earlier exercises, but that was all. A quick survey of the fixed equipment left behind was of considerable value and revealed that each cubicle was fitted out with a chart table, anglepoise lamps and an intercom. Also, a broadcasting system to allow instructions to be issued to all trainees at the same time was usable. Projection facilities in each control room, and background sound production in the form of recorded aeroengine noises, were there to come into play as required. The three of us now knew what amenities were readily available.

In the following days we planned the necessary alterations and additions and drew up new exercises that reflected the latest information available on operational flying, in addition to that gained by our own experience. We lost Peter Wright, for his commission came through, and now as a pilot officer there were other obligations for him; in his place we acquired Flight Sergeant Payne and Sergeant Kitt, both navigators. The extra pairs of hands was welcome. Each of the two instruction rooms would also have to double up as a briefing room; to this end wall maps of the whole of the air war area of Europe, down to the Mediterranean and to the extent of German-occupied territory to the East, were compiled and erected. In this way we could – in addition to their other uses – promote through the exercises an awareness of the placement of European cities and towns, so that the navigator could access them quickly on maps and charts should they be needed urgently at any time.

A point was reached when it was expedient and possible to open for business. We learned from the process and made adjustments as the early exercises were completed. We had already used the experience of the instrument specialists on the camp to modify the mechanism of the clocks, so that periods of low navigation activity could be speeded up and exercise flights of five hours or so could be covered in the actual three hours of the instructional period. Once under way the expected slow acceptance of this form of navigation instruction gradually increased, so that more staff was inevitable, and at the same time the individual course instructors gained a free morning or afternoon to prepare or develop their own particular role in the training programme.

For staff such as Len Waern and myself, living off the camp precincts, there was the advantage of being able to relax completely and enjoy the off-duty periods outside in the fresh air, which was most welcome after spending many working hours in a closed, darkened building. Daphne and I were tied to Wigtown for most of our home supplies, with Newton Stewart a few miles away for perhaps a wider range of shopping on a Saturday; consequently, we soon became well known to the local tradesmen. Len lived at a greater distance away with his family in a house on the coastal road, facing directly on to the sea in Luce Bay just south of Port William. We were invited to spend the occasional weekend with him, as was 'Chiefy' Payne and Kitt.

One morning, after I had been working with Len for some time, out of the blue he asked why I hadn't applied for a commission. I replied that I had been rebuffed on a previous occasion soon after I had returned from Gibraltar. His reply was to forget that and he would support my approach. I was just as ambitious as I had been before and promptly followed his advice and submitted my application. Interviews with the chief instructor and Group Captain D.I. Coote followed. I was fortunate with the station commander, for he had been the chief instructor at the time I joined the staff and now as the group captain I was not a stranger to him. About this time I had met two other warrant officers, one from Australia and the other from New Zealand, who had joined the instructional staff a short time earlier. During the period I was awaiting a date for my interview with the air officer commanding the group, they revealed that they were in the same position as myself. The appointments were fixed with little delay, and the result, as one might expect, was that they were all on the same morning at group headquarters near to Dumfries. We agreed that this required a stay in Dumfries overnight to meet the timings that we had to keep, and made our reservations at the County Hotel in the centre of town.

The afternoon to travel arrived and the four of us took the local train to Newton Stewart, where a change on to the mainline service rushed us to Dumfries. The evening passed pleasantly enough and an early start in the morning with the sun shining promised to be a good day. We were ready early for the taxi that had been booked and Daphne awaited our departure for the interviews before going forth to the shops. Looking out of the window to our room she said that there was a Rolls-Royce car outside the hotel entrance and perhaps it was our taxi. There was only one way to find out and that was to go down and enquire. Hat on, a last look in the long mirror, and down we went. My two companions were already in the foyer and indeed that car was our taxi. Saying goodbye to Daphne for the time being, two grey-blue and one dark-blue uniformed airmen climbed into the spacious rear of this magnificent vehicle. The driver already knew of our destination and we glided away on the next stage of a hoped-for advancement of careers in the air force. The journey was well timed as we swept into the drive of a large country house, stopping at open iron gates for permission to proceed. The guard had sprung to attention and saluted, which perhaps was due to the car rather than to three warrant officers inside. Our driver eventually pulled up at the foot of the steps to the main doors, allowing us to descend and make our entrance.

The hallway was large, with a staircase sweeping up to the first floor. The three of us were conducted to a waiting room. The building was quiet, almost as if we were the only people there, which of course was not so, as I was soon to find out. The door opened and my name was called – this was the moment everything depended on, convincing a senior officer

that I was just the right person to be promoted. I found the air commodore easy to talk to and ran through my experience in the service, adding
a brief note on my journey through occupied Belgium and France and
on to Gibraltar. My education drew some expression of surprise, in that
it had been based on engineering and technology, to be followed by my
thoughts on the work that I was now doing at RAF Wigtown. With the
final words that he would let me know after he had seen the other appli-
cants, he brought the interview to an end. The other two had much the
same recollection as myself. Our Rolls-Royce was still waiting for us at
the front steps, so we got in and left for the journey back to Dumfries,
feeling that the interviews had gone rather well, but that it was a case of
wait and see. By now Daphne was back at the hotel, where we enjoyed lunch
before boarding the train to take us back through the bleak countryside
of that part of Galloway to our Wigtown digs.

It was only a few days later that each of the three us was seen by the
group captain with the news that the applications had been successful, with
promotion to pilot officer rank, and to get kitted out with the correct
uniform. Normally leave was granted for this purpose, but in my case –
with the volume of use of our DR Trainer – I could only have the occasional day off to visit Dumfries to be measured and to have my uniform
and greatcoat made. Being unable to go down to London for a week was
perhaps an advantage, for Barbour's of Dumfries made a very respectable
job of the tailoring and everything else was available from the one shop
or in the town. I had been given a generous number of clothing coupons
and also an adequate allowance for the outfit. Daphne was pleased with
use of some of the spare coupons. In fact, with the further official issue
of coupons from time to time we had no further problem while they were
still required.

There was no ducking the situation – the coat of arms of a warrant
officer was of no use any more and the mess for this rank was now out
of bounds for me. It was now into the officers' mess or starve; well not quite,
as I had breakfast in our lodgings before leaving for the camp. However,
that initial visit did not turn out to be such an ordeal as expected, for I
had an experienced companion with me and some of the long-term
members welcomed me into the mess and put me at my ease. I introduced myself to the mess secretary and was booked in as a member. It

was as easy as that, but I still had to remind myself to tread carefully, for there were often unwritten rules to be followed.

It was not long after my entry into the officers' mess, and completion of my new kit and uniform, that I found my name on the list for orderly officer duties. On the appointed day I took over from the man who was coming off duty; I signed in and the first task was to check the books listed as secret and kept in the safe. Then followed a printed list of times and events that it was up to me to perform over the next twenty-four hours. I must say it all went very well, even when twice in the airmans' mess there had been no response to the loudly voiced question 'Any complaints?'.

In the morning towards the end of my tour of duty a potential disaster, for me, was avoided. All those in the training wing were paraded in the domestic camp before I marched them down to the working camp the other side of the airfield and lined them up on the parade square for the raising of the RAF flag. All was set ready for the ceremony when the correct command went right out of my head; I had heard it dozens of times but it wouldn't come back. This had to be resolved, so I strode down the line of men standing to attention, to the officer standing out in front and asked him to give the order as he was the senior officer on the parade. He didn't demur and promptly shouted out the command. It wasn't the correct order but it served the purpose of the moment and the standard party promptly raised the flag to its lofty position until sunset.

When leave became due, Daphne and I sometimes found it difficult to decide whether to stay in Scotland or to go down to London to see our families, mostly to Wembley where they both lived only a short walk away from each other. We could also visit other family members who lived in nearby areas. Of course, the entertainment in central London was readily available and with plenty of choice, certainly enough to satisfy our appetite. On one or two occasions, with one full week's leave ahead, the thought of the long train journey home became unattractive and a change of destination to Edinburgh was made. For me this was a new venue, but Daphne had been to the city several times, which made it easy to plan our days out from the Bruntsfield Hotel close to the Meadows. Lunch for these few days was mostly taken in local restaurants in the nearby university student area. It was in such circumstances – sitting there with Daphne, overhearing the chatter of groups of students and just noting their attitudes to the current situation – that it became obvious that their outlook was far removed from mine. Those students could only have been two years or so younger than me at the most and, yet, suddenly that small gap seemed to be a vast void. With my active wartime experiences, I considered myself so much of a different age that I could never feel part of their generation, nor they of mine.

Our training programme and methods in the simulation trainer had obviously been talked about away from our base, for the group navigation officer began to make his visits more frequently to discuss our aims and to add his comments. It was about this time that we were made aware of some new construction work being carried out in one of the hangars. A large, square perforation had been cut out of the thick concrete floor and a below-ground chamber constructed, some 6ft deep and lined with a concrete tank, complete with a drainage channel all round and a sump to collect any inflow of water and keep the floor dry. Above, a pre-fabricated building was being erected over the chamber. Our curiosity intensified when it was made known that our group would be involved in its use.

The new structure was high, for it could accommodate twenty trainees in four layers of cubicles, each fronted with glass and staggered one above the other so that each occupant had an unimpeded view of the white floor of the chamber below. The stairs reached to a further floor at the top of the building, upon which was a projection and tracking device together with a library of large glass transparencies of the whole of the British Isles, as seen from an aircraft in flight. The centre of the floor below was marked to indicate the position of the aircraft. The working surface for the operator above was a large sheet of plate glass that served as a support for the large glass transparencies being projected on to the white floor below. With this equipment we could simulate any route that was required in an exercise. Most of the airmen that were passing through our unit were direct from basic training in countries involved in the Empire Air Training Scheme, such as I had experienced myself in Canada, where the countryside was quite different to that of this country.

Len Waern, who by now had been promoted to flight lieutenant, was posted away on an investigatory trip to Canada and the United States for an extended period. Of course, he accepted with alacrity, but it was a breakup of our partnership, which had profited the two of us both during working hours and also socially. However, it was an assignment which, if offered, was not to be missed. I had already been promoted to flying officer rank and took over as the leader of the simulated navigation training unit. Len did keep in touch with us with a few short letters and postcards, which were welcomed. After an extensive tour of the United States he wrote to say that nothing in the training there was as advanced in our field as that which we had already developed.

With increased numbers of men being trained, the unit acquired more staff; among them Scotsman Flying Officer John Howett joined us. After a short time he had found accommodation in the village of Bladnoch for himself and his wife, and it was inevitable that, living close to each other and attending the same social functions, the two women should start a friendship that was to last many years into peacetime.

There was a constant flow of trainees passing through the Advanced Flying Unit (AFU), so postings in and out were commonplace, but such events were not frequent among the instructional staff. To quite a few this life was not at all unsatisfactory, but to the remainder there was a restless feeling that their experience and skill could be put to more active use. For months we were aware of unusual structures appearing along the coast south of Wigtown. In a bay close to Garlieston there was moored a floating concrete construction as big as a block of domestic flats, and further away towards Burrow Head a road on pontoons stretched out into the sea and was terminated by a bridgehead with what looked like skeletal steel pylons on each corner. These structures were all very visible from the air and became part of the coastal scene when flying out into the Irish Sea towards the Isle of Man. There was little doubt in our minds that this was experimental work towards seaborne landings somewhere. Surprisingly little was ever said about these monsters in the landscape; despite their prominence they were almost a secret.

Walking through the working camp one day I was overtaken by the adjutant on his bicycle. Slowing down he said: 'Good morning Gordon, can you drop into my office later this morning?' I confirmed that I would do that in about an hour or so if that was OK. With a nod of his head and 'See you then' he increased speed and disappeared around the corner of one of the buildings. As many of the days of May 1944 had slipped past without much variation in my programme, this was rather intriguing, but there was no point in being concerned about it now as there were other immediate matters to hand. But, as arranged, I presented myself at the door of his office, knocked and waited for his 'Come in.' I did so with the obligatory salute, ready to find out what he had to say.

'Ah, yes, you are being posted.'

'Oh right, on to a squadron?'

'No, no, it is only for two weeks to North Luffenham in Rutlandshire, to the Training Command Instructors School. They have gliders there too.' He gave me the dates of attendance and said they would route me through London, concluding with the remark: 'I expect Daphne would like to go home to her parents for a couple of weeks while you are away.' His comment was right on the ball; that man continued to surprise me, especially with the care he took to get to know the established staff of the camp. His advice and help was much appreciated, particularly when it involved families.

My visit home was fleeting and the train journey to the nearest station to North Luffenham prolonged, but a warm, sunny afternoon in the countryside was always pleasant, even if the railway buildings looked unoccupied except for a group of RAF men who had got off the train. One or two seemed to know each other, having probably met on the journey up. None of the officers were familiar to me, but that was soon resolved by making oneself known, having realised that we were all there for the same purpose. Transport arrived and took us up to the airfield and to what seemed to be two weeks of rather competitive effort. As might be expected, the whole range of information presentation was covered. This was a continuation of what had formed part of the staff navigation course taken previously at the Central Navigation School. Individual performance was required of each of us, not once but on several occasions on subjects that were given to you in advance. The resident lecturers made the assessment, but your companions attending had an input also, with no holds barred.

The sound of aircraft always seemed to be present in the skies of Rutlandshire; at no time was there a quiet period in the day. Then on the third or fourth day of our stay at North Luffenham the intensity of engine noise increased, as did the number of Dakota aircraft flying in the local area. In addition, they displayed new bands of white paint on the fuselage and wings – against the standard aircraft camouflage these symbols of identity screamed out to be noticed. It was obvious that some event was about to happen; the question was what, and that it must be big. This was 6 June 1944. At breakfast time the morning air was free of noise resounding around the heavens; it was nearly midsummer and it had been light for hours already. There was an air of anticipation but nobody had the answer as to why; if they had they were not saying. However, it was soon made public with an announcement over the Tannoy system – the invasion of mainland Europe had started. It was that big.

The long-awaited news was received with much enthusiasm, but each person on the course personally felt that they had 'missed the boat' in that they were in the wrong place at the time when an active involvement was desired. Nothing could change the situation, though, and all that could be done was to make the most of our current obligation. Of the remaining days, the programme designed for us continued to completion and the final hour or so was spent in discussing our personal results. The announcement of these could have given rise to a series of horror stories, but not so; as was often the case the outcomes were carried out in alphabetic order. Being one of the names in the middle of the alphabet I had time to wonder how my own showing would stand with the rest. Surprise, surprise, it was related that: 'If Flying Officer Mellor wishes to continue in this particular field and likes to get in touch with me after this war is over, I can assure him that a job will be available with me.' Well, well! That was a boost to anybody's confidence. I am not sure that I heard any comment about the remaining course members in the closing minutes. Back in London I rejoined Daphne. We packed our bags to go back 'abroad'. Where abroad? To Scotland of course! The local people in Wigtown would say that when their sons or daughters went over the border into England, especially if it was as far as London, then that was abroad to them. It was right that it worked in the reverse direction!

Gordon at Ans rail station in 2010.

Chapter 12

Now Light Your Fires

I was now back in post at Wigtown airfield and, like everyone else, keenly following the progress in France. The hold-up around Caen had been resolved and the Allies had at last relieved Paris. The national newspapers were full of pictures of the liberation celebrations. But I wondered how the people who gave me so much assistance had fared in the many months that had passed since October 1942. Indeed, were they even still there? For they could have disappeared without trace. Dédée – Andrée de Jongh – and her father were based in Paris and Robert and Germaine Aylé and Elizabeth Barbier were residents, as were many others. It was far too early for such intelligence, if there was any, to reach persons down at my level, or for any acknowledgement of their activities to be made known.

Navigators still under training continued to arrive from those countries involved in the Empire Air Training Scheme, to gain further experience, particularly of flying conditions around this country and northern Europe. To this end gen on new equipment and techniques was constantly sought. We were fortunate in this requirement, for Flying Officer Willie Humble maintained an information room that was a good source of the knowledge and facts that we required. In addition, our thoughts and plans ran far ahead of Europe, for when conflict there had been finally resolved there still would be the problems of Japan and the rest of the Far East. Maps and charts of that vast area and much information were on request.

It was at this time that Daphne and I felt considerable anxiety because of the introduction by the Germans of the V1, or flying bomb as it was known, being launched against the southern counties and London in particular. I knew that my mother was still using the Anderson shelter that had been delivered in the early days of autumn 1939. I had spent some time in digging out a rectangular pit in which to erect the frame and steel sheeting and then back-filling the soil over the exposed protective curved roof. It had been OK to start with, but in the second season the following year the water table lifted and the shelter filled with water and became unusable. Fortunately the local authority laid a concrete floor and walls of the same material to keep the water out, which was most successful. Now the shelter could be used indefinitely and was some protection. Our two families lived no more than 300yd apart and during a previous air raid a stick of bombs had landed along a road between the two houses, causing some damage to one of them. Despite the shelter protection, a V1 explosion at close quarters would be most devastating to life.

Soon after my taking on the duties of a pilot officer I had been approached through Len Waern with the idea of helping the local Air Training Corps (ATC). There was a squadron of boys all eager to progress, with just one man to do everything at the weekly meetings held in a small hall in Wigtown, only a short distance from where Daphne and I were living. I needed to know something of the assistance that was required and to meet the officer in charge of the unit to ensure that we could work together. Such a meeting was arranged and Pilot Officer Eakenhead and I spent an hour or so discussing the best way in which I could be a positive help. We got on together rather well. He, like many other ATC officers, was in a civilian occupation during the day and performed his other duties with the boys in his spare time. It was agreed that after the parade at the beginning of each meeting I should use the next three-quarters of an hour on mini lectures and talks about navigation, flying and all the varied matters and events commonplace in the air force. The resident officer-in-charge would then complete the remainder of the evening. The boys were keen, but I still tried to finish my section of the evening with them wanting to know just a bit more, so that we then had a starting point for the next occasion.

With the exception of John Wilkin, who I saw again during that short visit to RAF Finningley while coverting to Halifax aircraft on the squadron, and the unexpected meeting with Dicky Fairly and the Catalina in Gibraltar, I had not met anyone from my earlier days in the service.

When posted from Bournemouth not one person from the units that I had served with in this country, or in Canada, accompanied me to Lichfield. However, at last one such individual did arrive at RAF Wigtown to supplement the staff for a short period. He was Flying Officer Crompton-Batt, complete with a double Distinguished Flying Cross; the last time I had seen him was on our passing-out parade at RCAF Fingal in Ontario. We were not great friends but it was pleasant to meet up again.

Since we had arrived in Wigtown and made our first visit to meet Mrs Hawthorn, Robert's mother, at the schoolhouse at Ravenstone, we had made many more visits to see her; she was of course anxiously awaiting the return of her prisoner of war son.

The national newspapers in the early days of May 1945 were building up everybody's expectations of peace in Europe, to the point of it being highly probable within a few days. Daphne and I had vacated our lodgings in Fordbank House and a subsequent stay at a place called Beechwood, and for quite some time had been living in North Main Street in Wigtown, which formed one side of the main square of the town. It was there that most celebrations and local events took place. After midnight, at an early hour of the morning of 8 May 1945, a sudden explosion of amplified music erupted into the country silence under the windows of our bedroom, obviously with the intention of waking up all the inhabitants of the surrounding houses, hotels and shops. Shouted enquiries to the perpetrators of this outburst of sound, Gordon Henry and his companions, revealed that today was Victory in Europe Day, better known as VE Day. It also was a work day and I had to be down at the camp at 08.00 hours. After a decent interval it was necessary to shut the windows, draw the curtains and to try and get some sleep for what turned out to be a very short night.

Within days Robert Hawthorn had been repatriated and sent off home on leave, but I was unable to see him for some time owing to him suffering with jaundice brought about by a sudden improvement in his diet after the rather limited value of food eaten while a prisoner of war. However, he recovered well and we did have a weekend together in his own home. I remember that when Daphne and I made that first visit to see him, I wore civilian clothes in order to play down how fortune had favoured me while leaving him at almost a standstill. He was a warrant officer by now, though. At our reunion I found out that, way back in October 1942, after landing by parachute, the movement and rustling I had heard in the field of cabbages had been him, neither of us thinking that we could have landed so close together. With the two of us believing the other to be the enemy, it was a game of 'hide-and-seek' of a serious kind and a question of who had the most patience. After moving off he had walked into a village and, seeing a house showing a little light, had knocked on the door. He was invited in by a man who declared himself to be the mayor and promised to help. How far Robert had walked I cannot recall, but it was still dark at the time; the sky must still have been reflecting the glow from the aircraft blaze on the ground. The mayor's promise did not materialise, but two officers from the Luftwaffe camp at Saint-Trond did and he was taken into custody.

A short while after Robert's reappearance I received a telephone message from another survivor from our crew; this time it was Harry Richards, who had filled the mid-upper gunner's position. He wanted to come up to Wigtown from South Wales to see both Robert and myself, and to bring his brother with him – could Daphne and I put them both up for two or three nights? Of course the answer was yes. They arrived tired after a long train journey, but a meal revived their spirits and Harry's story of his last few minutes in the Halifax was quite brief, as was his descent to the ground, for the plane had lost more height and he had landed heavily in a tree close to Mopertingen a small village just to the west of where Robert and I came down. In the event he had suffered a seriously broken leg, leaving him helpless until found and taken to hospital in Maastricht for a stay of many weeks. This was followed by a further spell in a hospital in Düsseldorf and then a long period in the POW camp. He considered the medical treatment he had received to have been very good.

I was on duty during the days that they were staying with us but we had my off-duty times together. Both Harry and his brother visited Robert at Ravenstone on one day of their visit. I also learned from Harry that the other survivors of the crew – namely radio operator Doug Giddens and the second pilot Mark Mead – were each picked up in daylight and sent to Stalag Luft VIIIB. Later information indicated that flight engineer

George Green's parachute did not have enough height or time to open properly and he tragically fell on to a house just beyond Harry Richards's landing place. It is thought that despite the fire, Eddie Edwards, the pilot, was trying to land the plane – with Norman McMaster in it with him – in nearby fields on Op het Root close to Rosmeer. A few seconds between each of us had made the difference between life and death. Finally, all the crew of Halifax PM-Q had been accounted for.

Returned prisoners of war began to arrive in groups for short refresher courses; some of them were not happy men. I felt that they had not realised that the country had a commitment to continue in the Far East and that this could be a long-term affair. The knowledge of these navigators obviously varied, depending on when they had been imprisoned; those from a more recent time were more up to date than those from earlier in the war, for there had been many advances in Bomber Command over the years. Most of the time during lectures, exercises or talks the odd outburst could be treated sympathetically. Most of them had experienced a rough time. However, on just one or two occasions their input reached a very personal level, which wasn't acceptable. With an understanding approach it was soon over and forgotten.

In the beginning of August 1945 the new name of 'Hiroshima' exploded upon the ears and eyes of the world, to be followed three days later by another city's name, 'Nagasaki'. The majority of us were well aware this time just where that town was situated and there was no doubt in our minds of the enormity of each attack. Then, all hostilities were planned to cease on the 15th of that month. Excellent news as it indeed was, down at the airfield speculation was voiced as to what effect the peace would have upon us. Imaginations had plenty of opportunity to be exercised.

VE Day had been a boisterous, noisy, exuberant celebration in the centre of town, for many families had sons, daughters or husbands in the forces in Europe, even in the Middle East, and it all seemed to be close to home. In contrast, on VJ Day the celebrations were more controlled and perhaps more of a muted, if satisfying, nature, for Japan was so far away. The night-time bonfire right on top of the hill above town was huge. The flare of the fire was meant to be seen right across the water to the other side of Wigtown Bay. The smell of burned wood hung over the town all the next day. Fortunately, because it was not within the experience of the townsfolk, I did not think it likely that they would connect that smell with the huge palls of smoke that hung over many continental cities, and indeed over London and other large towns in this country after a major night bombing raid.

Having a spare bedroom in our lodgings seemed to act like a magnet and attracted visitors for several days at a time. The first was Daphne's brother, Ken, who had returned to the UK after nearly five years' service in Palestine, Egypt and the Sudan; we soon re-established our friendship, dating back to schooldays. Her other brother, Geoffrey, in the RAMC, was posted to Lockerbie for a brief term, which enabled us to travel to meet him in Dumfries. Daphne's parents had made the journey twice – the first time had an interesting touch to it. We had arranged to meet them at the railway station in Newton Stewart on arrival and to travel on the train to Wigtown together. While walking up to the station we heard a loud shriek on the whistle of the train, which caused us to rush on to the footbridge over the tracks to reach the platform, only to see the train passing under the bridge with my father-in-law leaning out of the carriage waving frantically to us. Moments later, the train came to a screeching halt and waited for us to run along the track and climb up into the carriage where our visitors were seated. A gesture out of the window indicated to the driver that all was well. On arrival at our destination I nipped along the platform to thank the driver for stopping for us. Now, where else would you have received that sort of consideration except on a local branch line?

Judy Matheson, a nurse who had attended Daphne while in Creswell Hospital in Dumfries, came several times in response to invitations to receptions in the officers' mess on the camp. Which reminds me that we had as an honorary member of the mess a rather splendid figure, when in full Highland dress, of James Robertson Justice, not so well known then as a film actor as in later years, but who undoubtedly was an impressive local resident who fished in the River Bladnoch.

All serving at the airfield were not kept in suspense for long, for plans must have been made a considerable time in advance, in anticipation of victory. RAF Wigtown was to close down shortly. The incoming of new trainees slowed and then stopped completely. Those already passing through, having completed their course both on the ground and in the air, were posted away. And then there were none. It became a task of winding up the training branch of the camp so that all was left in order; much had to be returned to stores or to the salvage dump. The other branches of the service that made a station active were doing the same, and some postings began to come through. On 19 October 1945 the officers' mess held its last dance, attended by many local friends who lived within the distance of a car ride. It was a good, colourful crowd and many a reel was performed with varying ability and vigour.

The October days were beginning to shorten and still there was no idea where I was likely to be sent. Then salvation appeared on the scene in the form of Len Waern, now a squadron leader. I had not seen him since he'd gone to Canada and the United States. There were still two young Canadian officers in my team and his arrival gave them the opportunity to recall their own memories of places he had also visited. After a prolonged discussion he asked where our placements would be when RAF Wigtown closed its doors. The latest information was that we would most probably be sent on leave and the destination forwarded to our home address. He seemed to expect this answer, and then revealed that he was the chief navigation officer at No. 10 Air Navigation School (ANS) at RAF Chipping Warden, which was not far out from Banbury, and would I be interested in going there and setting up a DR Trainer such as we had developed before? It did mean starting from scratch, with just the bare accommodation. I expressed a keen interest and said yes. He was pleased and said he would put in a request for my posting.

The expected period of leave proved to be more than speculation and in fact departures became commonplace; mine started on 4 November for a period of two weeks. Some of my colleagues had already gone, without knowing their ultimate destination; more were left behind. It was hoped that we would all meet up again. In truth this was very doubtful. Daphne and I had already sent off by rail a large wooden box with most of our clothes and gear in it, to arrive at my home address in Wembley.

On the morning of our departure Daphne and I walked down to the railway station for the last time, making sure that we were on time on this occasion, as was the local train to Newton Stewart. With one last look towards the airfield not far away, we were gone. The railway journey was familiar to both of us – we had spent hours at various times watching the countryside flow past while talking or glancing through the newspapers. This time I must admit I just sat back, thinking over the events and times that had filled my days and some nights on and off duty while at Wigtown. In particular I appreciated the relationships with many of the residents of the town, who had welcomed the men and women of the air force into their lives.

The effort put in at the RAF Central Navigation School had proved to be well worth while, for I had been favoured with an excellent posting. It was busy but interesting and responsible work, with an advancement in rank, for promotion was due in just a few weeks. In addition, Daphne and I had been fortunate enough to spend extended periods together, which had been denied to all but a small number of servicemen and women.

I suppose that some of the time on that long train journey I was just daydreaming. However, I did recall that when Daphne was staying in Wigtown for some time, that in total we had a lived in five different accommodations. After the first few days at the Commercial Hotel, owned by Mr and Mrs Macrae, we had gone to rooms with the MacMasters in the country house named Fordbank down on the Bladnoch Road. Then to Beechwood with Mrs Janet McCoupland, who was the bailie or mayor of the town. Later on we had a short spell at Croft an Rie, opposite the Site of the Martyrs on the low-level fields that flooded during periods of high tides. Finally, there was a flat at 21 North Main Street, right at the centre of the town community.

And yet, despite all the activity recalled of that time, as we sped south from Dumfries, it was impossible to forget that on two occasions we had to rush Daphne from Wigtown by ambulance some 60 miles into Creswell Hospital in Dumfries. Much to our dismay, neither of the hoped-for new members of the family survived. They have remained for ever in Scotland.

Bomber Command veteran navigator Gordon Mellor.

Chapter 13

Surplus to Requirements

After a few days home in Wembley, despite the many comforts, advantages and family company, which was all very enjoyable, I felt rather unsettled. Probably due to waiting for the posting decision to be resolved and possibly the fact that some of the people with low demobilisation numbers had already left their RAF service life behind them; my number had still some time to go before it became operative, but change was in the air. I was still keen to get on with the job and in the back of my mind was the thought of trying to stay in the service.

The large, sealed wooden box dispatched from Wigtown well before we left had not been delivered, and many enquiries at the railway goods office failed to reveal what had happened to it. Eventually it was declared lost and the only avenue left to us was to claim on the insurance. Some of the contents had to be returned to RAF stores or paid for; certainly my uniform overcoat was an expensive loss. The box was obviously stolen, for an attempt had been made to open it when my brother originally sent it up to us by the same method.

Just before the two weeks' leave expired a telegram arrived. I thought, 'This is it', but it wasn't, for it was an extension of leave of another seven days, which would take me up to almost the end of November. Of course, Daphne and the rest of the family were happy with this message and I enjoyed the outcome of it too. Leave was largely home life, but we did see a couple more shows up in town and on one occasion, while passing through Leicester Square, Daphne met an old friend from her own days at His Majesty's Theatre. This was not a common event; in fact the only previous occasion had been while on Crewe station on a Sunday afternoon when theatrical touring companies were moving from one location to another.

The next telegram arrived after a few days with the instruction to report to No. 10 ANS at Chipping Warden in Northamptonshire, just as Len Waern had promised. This was great and the only posting for me that had been specially arranged other than that following my return from Belgium. However, there would prove to be a twist in its tail.

So it was that 27 November 1945 saw me travelling to Banbury by train and getting a lift out to the airfield. The settling-in process didn't take long even though the camp was full. I would have to share available accommodation just outside the camp boundary with other officers, but as it was only a couple of minutes' walk to the mess it was not a problem. That evening Len Waern and I renewed contact in the mess and, after being introduced to other members of staff, I was made aware of the variation to the posting. On 1 December the whole of the personnel of this camp were moving to RAF Swanton Morley in Norfolk – engineers, clerks, aircrew, aircraft, motor transport, the lot – and until we were all there in new quarters there was not a lot for me to do except help others to pack their equipment.

Strangely, mail for me began to arrive immediately and among it there was an official-looking envelope, sent out under the Chief of Air Staff, Lord Portal's signature. It revealed that an organisation was to be set up to recognise, aid and maintain contact with all those in the occupied territories who had assisted airmen to evade or escape capture. The question being asked now was, would we the escapers support this venture for as long as it took? Of course one would; our indebtedness to these people was immense and a letter of acceptance was posted off immediately. Ernest Dales, a serving officer, had already been appointed to act as secretary.

On the first day of December the move to Swanton Morley took place. The Wellington aircraft were flown direct to the new airfield, but the majority of personnel travelled by train overnight. Barring a few minor problems, for most of us it worked superbly well; the planning must have been practical and possible. We could now get settled in and get to work. As we had experienced at Chipping Warden, accommodation was at a premium and although most of the buildings were pre-war, the officers' mess was not large enough to provide all officers with a separate room and a number, including myself, shared a former barrack room. Space was adequate, though, it was clean and the paintwork in good condition;

importantly, the heating and hot water were first rate. Attached to each sizeable barrack room was a single room that was not very big, but adequate, and it gave one person his privacy. Our one was already occupied, but I intended to keep an eye on it should there be a vacancy. And there was eventually.

Next morning it was down to the squadron leader's office for information on the building we were to convert into a navigation training unit. Making my first visit with Len Waern I found it to be more substantial than I had expected. Internally, the floor area had been simply divided up into two large rooms with a central entrance area in between. One of these rooms had an office within its space; I thought straightaway: 'That is for me, at the centre of what happens here.' After a good look round came the question from Len: 'Well what do you think?' The building had previously been the armoury, conveniently divided up. Indeed, it was ideal – it was clean and warm and the long work benches against the walls could be adapted for our use. To answer his question it was only necessary to say 'OK.' Obviously he had a good idea himself of what needed to be done, so he was prepared to tell me that we could request materials from the construction and maintenance depot, but they could not supply any labour for they were already busy themselves; we would have to do it all. Well, not quite all. A service carpenter and two NCOs would be made available, and some trainees until the air navigation courses started again. I commented to Len that it was a pity we hadn't 'Chiefy' Payne and Sergeant Kitt still with us from Wigtown. His answer was that there was a limit on what he could do. He gave me the keys to the building and said 'It is all yours' and left. There was a table and chair in the small room so I had a base to work from, and after a good look round a plan of work could be outlined. My small staff and a number of young workers also put in an appearance, all getting the message of 'Let's get on with it', for the construction work was going to take some time.

Much to my amazement I discovered that I was not the only staff navigator to turn up from the Wigtown group; within a couple of days of arrival I had need to speak with the new mess secretary and found that it was 'Duke' Warren, who had been one of the course commanders previously. I found the many new acquaintances in the mess had discussed the future extensively and the general current opinion had considerable impact on my thoughts on the subject. I soon learned that now the war was over careers in the RAF were going to be limited and at best one could not expect more than a short-term engagement, perhaps of up to two years. If discharge was then enforced, which was not unlikely, we would be those two years behind everybody else in continuing their former peacetime careers. Bearing all this in mind, at the first opportunity for two or three days' leave I went home and visited the surveying partnership that I had worked for up to the time of joining the RAF in 1940, to sound out their interest. Mind you, they were under an obligation to reinstate you upon your release from the services. However, they did not need such coercion for they were quite willing for me to return. The money was not going to be great, but we would be able to manage for a time.

With a double room available at the King's Head Hotel in East Dereham, Daphne was able to come up for the house warming party and dance at the mess on 1 February 1946. She was warmly welcomed both by Len Waern and Duke Warren, who she had known for quite some time. The party went on, so that it was the early hours before the coach delivered us back at the hotel. We had both enjoyed the occasion, but I often wondered if she felt the loss of the company of the many people she knew in the theatre, even though I never saw any sign of regret at leaving it all behind her.

My promotion to flight lieutenant was published in the supplement to the London Gazette, which pleased me. We had done well with the development of the new trainer – the briefing room was finished and fitted out with wall maps and furniture, and the benches previously used for maintaining armaments were now resurfaced and suitable for working with charts and maps. The remaining work continued, even while training was beginning to press forward.

I was beginning to receive letters from one or two helpers in Belgium and France, sent to my home address and passed on to Swanton Morely, but nothing from close friends. My attempts to establish the whereabouts of Michael Joyce had not been successful; only a whisper had come my way that he had been at RAF Valley for a time. Nothing from John Wilkin, with whom I had had a brief meeting back in the summer of 1942; it was possible he had not survived ops. Further back, there was absolutely no word on John King, who had been my flying partner during training. Nor with Don Jennings from Tasmania, who came to Wembley for our wedding in July 1943. Ah, well, no doubt information would be more readily available as months or years went by.

I received a call from station headquarters. My release number had been posted, my time had come – I had to wind up my duties and report to RAF Uxbridge. Somebody else would now have to complete what I had started. The whole release operation ran smoothly for it had been working for some time and as far as I was aware there was no provision for delay. It seemed to take just an hour or so to be processed. Then it was time to make one's goodbyes, pack, and then you were outside the gates of the airfield and on your way. That was the significant moment: the cutoff point of all that had filled the last six years. You were now surplus to requirements.

The departure station was East Dereham for a train to London and then the suburban rail service to Wembley. A night's sleep at home and thenceforth off in the morning by train to No. 1 Depot, RAF Uxbridge. Out of Uxbridge station it was a left turn down the High Street and, a short way along the Hillingdon Road, was the entrance to the RAF Depot. There was a familiar feeling passing through those gates; I had done this before. Could it really be years ago and not weeks? Other men looked as if they were going in the right direction, so I decided to follow them. Hmm, this was it. A neat suite of rooms and a neat suite of people to see you out. Perhaps I should give this place its correct title of 'The Personnel Detachment, Dispersal Centre'. Well here I was, ready to be dispersed. 'Name and number?' the official asked. 'Mellor, 172802.' 'Yes sir, we have you on our list.' A few notes were made, and the relevant papers, including instructions regarding civil employment, were handed to me. Finally, I was advised that a coach would be leaving in a few minutes to take me and others to the clothing distribution centre at Wembley.

There was not much chat in the coach as familiar suburbia slipped past the plate-glass windows; the twin towers of the stadium rose up ahead and the coach turned off Empire Way and came to a halt in front of the former Olympic swimming pool. Inside it was one vast floor area, not a drop of water in sight, but there was an orderly display of all types of civilian clothing; one was reminded immediately that it looked like a huge Burton's tailoring shop. The choice was yours, with plenty of advice to hand, so you gathered up a collection of items to make up an outfit, all the right size of course. There were empty tables to allow you to pack everything in a suitable cardboard container provided. There was then only a short walk to the bus stop, a single ride on a No. 83 bus to the end of my road and I would be home.

While packing up my choice of clothing into the box, I had a companion at the same table, a long-serving leading aircraftman, who started telling me some outrageous yarn with a straight face. At one point I laughed out loud, and his face broke out into a broad grin as he hurried off to the exit with his box. He had made the most of what had been his very last chance to pull the leg of someone who had been of a more senior rank. I had been caught out all right, and why not? Were we not the same? Now we were both just 'Misters' weren't we? I left the clothing centre and climbed aboard the local bus. The conductress refused my fare and at my destination wished me luck as I stepped down to the pavement.

My last day of RAF service was 15 May 1946.

Postscript

With the ending of active service and return to civilian life in 1946, it would be natural to feel that the story had come to an end, but this was not so. For there was – through the Royal Air Forces Escaping Society – an ongoing connection with those of the occupied countries who had risked everything to help us in our endeavours to return to Allied territory. Europe and other Second World war centres were battered and desperate; it was now the turn of the escapers and evaders jointly to try and aid any of their helpers in need. At the end of the timescale of fifty years in 1995, demand had diminished to a very low level and the society closed its books.

However, relationships had strengthened and the membership wished to retain their connection with their international friends. Shortly afterwards, Roger Stanton sprang to the forefront to organise a new society to encompass all three services and members from SOE and FANY under the title of the WW2 Escape Lines Memorial Society, abbreviated to ELMS. It still has a close connection with its continental counterparts, with Eden Camp Modern History Theme Museum and its membership, which is spread worldwide. The many wartime trails are being followed by the original escapees and helpers, and members of their families – sons and daughters and adult grandchildren.

In July 2007, serving officers of the Royal Air Force, accompanied by Bob Frost and myself, visited Dédée (Andrée de Jongh), founder and chief of the Comète line, in hospital. It was one of those rare moments to remember always; sadly, barely three months later, in October, Dédée died, and once again Bob and I made another visit to Brussels to attend with many others her funeral service at l'Abbaye de la Cambre.

The aims and objects of the original organisations are still being retained and the relationships forged in the 1940s are stronger than ever, for the debt owed to the helpers has still to be paid in full.

A Final Word

I am grateful to Mr Alfred Huberman, vice chairman of the executive committee of the Bomber Command Association for recalling the following significant quotation made by Marshal of the Royal Air Force, Sir Arthur Harris, Commander-in-Chief of Bomber Command: 'No one will ever know what it took to climb into a bomber and fly for hundreds of miles over enemy territory, through all hazards of the weather and the enemy defences, which brought crews to the brink of mental and physical exhaustion.'

Index